ABOUT THE EDITORS

Dr. Frank J. Menolascino, Professor of Psychiatry and Pediatrics at the University of Nebraska Medical Center, Omaha, has long been concerned with bettering the quality of life for Nebraska's mentally retarded and mentally ill citizens. Since his residency days, he has fought against institutional neglect, as an individual and as a consultant to institutions, organizations, and the mental health system. As a member of the 1968 Governor's Citizens' Study Committee on Mental Retardation, he helped construct a six-year plan to better the quality of life for Nebraska's mentally retarded citizens. The Nebraska Plan has received both national and international attention as a prototype for developing and implementing the normalization concept throughout an actual delivery of services system. Among his numerous publications, Dr. Menolascino has edited *Psychiatric Aspects of the Diagnosis and Treatment of Mental Retardation*, Special Child Publications, 1972.

The background of Dr. Paul H. Pearson reflects a strong awareness of the diverse factors that affect mental retardation. He is involved in various professional organizations concerning cerebral palsy, epilepsy, and pediatrics. In 1966-67 he served as Special Assistant to the United States Surgeon General. The previous year he was Assistant Program Director of the Mental Retardation Program with the National Institute of Child Health and Human Development. Currently, Dr. Pearson is Director with the Meyer Children's Rehabilitation Institute in Omaha, Nebraska. His ideas and research have appeared in several periodicals and publications.

BEYOND THE LIMITS

INNOVATIONS IN SERVICES FOR THE SEVERELY AND PROFOUNDLY RETARDED

Edited by

Frank J. Menolascino, M.D. *and* **Paul H. Pearson, M.D.**

Photographs by

Robert Coleman

With a Foreword by

Robert B. Kugel, M.D.

Special Child Publications

These papers, revised and updated in 1973-74, were presented at the Conference on Severely Retarded-Multiply Handicapped in 1972, at the University of Nebraska Medical Center, Omaha, Nebraska.

© 1974
SPECIAL CHILD PUBLICATIONS
A Division of Bernie Straub Publishing Co., Inc.
4535 Union Bay Place N.E.
Seattle, Washington 98105

2nd printing, July 1975
3rd printing, June 1976

Standard Book Number: 0-87562-053-1
Library of Congress Catalog Card Number: 74-84668

Printed in the United States of America

FOREWORD

A major role of an institution of higher learning is to provide continuing education programs that are highly relevant to emerging trends of knowledge. This book directly addresses itself to both the existing and emerging trends in our storehouse of knowledge for effectively helping severely retarded-multiply handicapped youngsters. International and national trends are reviewed with particular reference to those attitudinal, programatic, and management techniques which hold great promise for directly aiding handicapped young citizens.

Robert B. Kugel
Dean, College of Medicine
University of Nebraska Medical Center

Paul H. Pearson, M.D.   Frank J. Menolascino, M.D.

PREFACE

This publication is the result of a recent Conference at the University of Nebraska Medical Center on current-future challenges in providing services for severely retarded-multiply handicapped citizens. The timeliness of this topic is reflected in the growing tide of interest and involvement in this human service area.

Unfortunately, there are still many who believe that severely retarded individuals are incapable of any learning—even in acquiring such basic skills as eating and dressing. This traditional perception is in sharp contrast to the presentations herein, since they all underscore that the severely retarded-multiply handicapped are capable of becoming independent in areas such as basic self-help skills, behavioral control, language development, and motor mobility.

Since many have underestimated the developmental potentials of these children, they have often been excluded from public schools. Hence the parents of such children are often unable to find the services which their children so direly need, and are generally forced to choose among only three possibilities: 1) Keeping their child at home without adequate professional services; 2) Relying on the preciously few available local services which are typically provided by associations for retarded children or in University settings; and 3) Placement of their children in public or private institutions. The belief has also been a longstanding rationale for the need of custodial institutional services.

Fortunately, today we no longer have to say that custodial care programs in large institutional settings provide the major source of services for the severely retarded-multiply handicapped. Indeed, these institutional settings have undergone major attitudinal changes (as reviewed by Dr. Grunewald), and cross disciplinary-cross modality programming approaches can provide specific treatment interventions (as discussed by Mrs. Haynes). The implementation of these contemporary program ingredients and expectations for multi-handicapped citizens demand a new look at the basic values and related goals of services delivery systems—a topic which is directly addressed by Drs. Keith and Sage.

The majority of these citizens can now live at home if there are sufficient appropriate developmental and family social services in the community to meet individual and family needs. These latter dimensions are reviewed by Drs. Galloway and Menolascino in this publication. Lastly, the long-standing need for manpower in this specialized area of mental retardation services, and guidelines for filling this need, are underscored by Dr. Pearson.

Accordingly, the thrust of this Conference Proceedings publication is to provide a current progress note on the attitudinal, programmatic, and treatment-management changes which have revitalized this area of human service. These considerations hold much promise for extending the developmental horizons for a group of our retarded citizens who have for so long been neglected. *(Editors)*

CONTRIBUTORS

Robert Coleman
Photographer, Mental Health Educator
University of Nebraska Medical Center
Omaha, Nebraska

Charles Galloway, Ph.D.
Director, Child Development Services
Eastern Nebraska Community Office of Retardation
Omaha, Nebraska

Karl Grunewald, M.D.
Head of Division for the Care of the Mentally Retarded
National Board of Health and Welfare
Stockholm, Sweden

Una Haynes, R.N., M.P.H.
Associate Director and Nurse Consultant
Professional Services Program Department
United Cerebral Palsy Associations, Inc.
New York, New York

Kenneth D. Keith, Ph.D.
Director of Planning and Research
Beatrice State Home
Beatrice, Nebraska

Robert B. Kugel, M.D.
Dean, College of Medicine
University of Nebraska Medical Center
Omaha, Nebraska

Frank J. Menolascino, M.D.
Professor of Psychiatry and Pediatrics
University of Nebraska Medical Center
Omaha, Nebraska
        and
Senior Vice-President
National Association for Retarded Citizens

Paul H. Pearson, M.D.
Meyer Professor of Child Health
Director, Meyer Children's Rehabilitation Institute
University of Nebraska Medical Center
Omaha, Nebraska
        and
Member, National Developmental Disabilities Council

Hugh M. Sage, Ph.D.
Director, Hospital Improvement Project
Beatrice State Home
Beatrice, Nebraska

CONTENTS

INTERNATIONAL TRENDS IN THE CARE OF THE SEVERELY-PROFOUNDLY RETARDED AND MULTIPLY HANDICAPPED

Introduction (Frank Menolascino)

Our keynote speaker for this Conference is Dr. Karl Grunewald. Karl visited Nebraska in 1969 at the beginning of the Nebraska Plan for the Mentally Retarded. At that time we fully experienced his direct and extremely helpful approaches to assessing programs for the retarded. His past and current professional roles are a significant model of how his posture of meaningful help for the retarded came to fruition. Karl Grunewald was born in Herald County in Sweden, 51 years ago. He received his Doctor of Medicine in 1948, and began his training in Child Psychiatry at that time. Shortly thereafter he became very active in mental retardation as a member of the World Health Organization, the International League for the Retarded, and the Swedish Association for Retarded Children (the F.U.B.). It was a natural next step that when Sweden elected to initiate a more dynamic approach towards its retarded citizens, Karl Grunewald was selected to lead the National Division of Mental Retardation. Since that time, Karl has discussed, written, and most importantly, initiated excellent programs of help for the retarded citizens of his country during the last twelve years as Director of the Division of Mental Retardation in Sweden. Surprisingly, he has done all of these activities while simultaneously representing both the advocates of the retarded (the Swedish ARC) and what he terms the "politicals" (governmental officials)—a remarkable accomplishment! However, he has not accomplished this task by being evasive to parents or vague to the "politicals." Rather, he has actively worked with both parties to seek a consensus as to what was needed, and then how best to obtain same. He has shown great foresight in designing programs for the retarded which *do* deliver service, while at all times being mindful of alternatives, costs, and monitoring. Those of us who have had the opportunity to know him can attest to the range and depth of his knowledge, and the deep humanistic posture that accompanies same. It is my pleasure to introduce our keynote speaker, Dr. Karl Grunewald.

INTERNATIONAL TRENDS IN THE CARE OF THE SEVERELY-PROFOUNDLY RETARDED AND MULTIPLY HANDICAPPED
Karl Grunewald

The severe and profoundly retarded have traditionally been

considered incapable of obtaining significant benefits from either

medical therapy or from psychological assessment and activity.

It is not surprising, therefore, that this particular group of the

retarded have received so little attention from either physicians

or psychologists. This group of patients were frequently con-

sidered as an interesting category for research, but they were

less attractive as objects of medical care and treatment -- with

the usual approach being a system of passively providing for

them and their needs. Much of the behavior currently found

among the severe and profoundly retarded is not characteristic

of their "retardedness", but the raw consequence of the lack

of programs which these individuals have experienced during

their developmental periods. They have been grossly subjected

to deviating and abnormal environments, and we could speak

about whose retardation these tragic consequences reflect at

this time since they are a result of deficiencies in their envir-

onment, the traditions of life created by society, the attitudes

of their parents, professionals, and so on. It is therefore, not

astonishing that over the world we are interested and engaged in seeking new approaches, and ask "What can we do for the severe and profoundly retarded?" I shall review some of these international topics and trends.

First of all we find that severe and profoundly retarded children or adults, even though many of them are in need of medical care, do not necessarily need to be cared for in an environment which is designed on a medical model. Instead, it has become clear that we can provide the medical care which they may need in housing which is designed and programmed around social and developmental activities.

Secondly, we find that the severe and profoundly retarded need to live in small groups (i. e. , groups involved in dining, recreational, and sleep activities with not more than 8 to 10 persons together). Yet we typically find that we always come in too late to the picture. We must start our habilitation earlier, so that the retarded are not just sitting around idly as passive consumers in meaningless situations which have been created from the neglect they have received from other experts or from society. This is very much the situation we find ourselves in on the international scene today, and it is characteristic that we today have what can be called a "lost generation" of the retarded

-- a generation who did not get much of anything from the psychological and habilitative point of view especially in contrast to what we can today provide to our severe and profoundly retarded citizens.

These problems have very much been improved by choosing the multi-disciplinary team approach, which means that now we can join together to resolve complex challenges and tasks where you can say that the members of the team together will know a lot and if they cooperate together they can promote new developmental horizons for the retarded. This approach and attitude of the multi-disciplinary team is not very widely accepted across the world in the care of the profoundly and severely retarded, since it is still mainly practiced within the medical model and it is very difficult to extend that model into community programs. However, there are many recent international trends toward extending this needed multi-disciplinary model beyond the confines of medical settings. I view this as an extremely positive trend since we need all the experts working together!

Another international trend is the establishment of special wards for multi-handicapped persons at ordinary hospitals. I have noted examples of annexed special wards to Children's

16

Hospitals, and an approach to long term care wherein the same team of professionals who confirm the diagnosis must now take the responsibility for providing local treatment and management. Pediatricians have not done that earlier, and tended to just convince the parents that there is nothing to do for their child except that he be placed in an institution elsewhere. This trend of integration of the special wards for long term care at children's hospitals provides a direct connection and responsibility for diagnostic clinics to also help the parents with the treatment-management consequences of the diagnosis obtained.

I want to stress that it is really important to observe that if we truly want an improved long range situation than we have now inherited much preventive work can be done to lower the number of severe and profoundly retarded children. You may have wondered how the situation is in the underdeveloped countries and what they do with all of their handicapped children. One approach is that they don't do anything, and the children die. Therefore, they do not have the problem of multi-handicapped children in underdeveloped countries. In developing countries which have not developed as far as our two countries have done, but are still open and developing, you will find that the rates of stillbirths and infant mortality have decreased successfully and that many children are saved. Yet, no one takes care of these children and though they are still saved to have a life, they are not habilitated or activated. This provides a situation wherein we then have a gap between rapidly growing diagnostic services and a great paucity of service delivery possibilities in child care for these children. The children are not activated and in fact they are merely kept alive through antibiotics and supportive medical care. Thus these countries have many children who are severe and profoundly retarded, and they live longer and longer. This is the exact situation we had about 20 to 30 years ago in Sweden, and we find today that we have a peak of severe and profoundly retarded young adults, of which the oldest are about in that age when the antibiotics were introduced (i.e., 25 to 30 years old, and the youngest of them are now 8 to 15 years old). They come from before the years that we started the more active habilitation programs, and this group of severely-profoundly retarded are the tragic result of life saving which was not followed by developmental activation, and they represent the "lost generation" of the retarded that I mentioned earlier.

I think that in your country, most of the states are in an

intermediate position now between the underdeveloped and developing nations. Judging from what I have seen during my visits to the U.S.A., I think that you have an astonishingly high number of severe-profoundly retarded children and young adults in your mental retardation hospitals. To be blunt, I have not seen any country with so many bedridden mentally retarded patients as I have seen in some states here in America. I was surprised, and did some comparisons of the number of the bedridden and the severely-profoundly retarded in Sweden and in Nebraska. I found that in Sweden, of all of our mentally retarded (30,000) we have only 1% who are bedridden -- from the youngest one to the oldest one. In contrast, Wolfensberger compiled a figure for your state and he noted that it was 4%. Now we can argue and edit this 4% figure or our 1% figure, and say that those are only the ones which are known by the local authorities. For example, it may be that there were still more who were being taken care of in other facilities or who were in their homes. In any event, the compilations are just a trial to find out where we are at this time. Perhaps "bedridden" is only a symptom, and behind each known bedridden patient there may be 10 times as many who are less bedridden but still are very severe   and/or profoundly retarded. However,

I think we can say that in your country you must pass to the next stage and that is to start habilitation programs earlier, and you can never do that without total connection between early intervention for children when they are born and closely follow them as newborn children.

As you know, the majority of the severely and profoundly retarded children are able to be diagnosed at least in the first months or in the first year of their lives. Even if you do early post-natal follow-up, you will find that your rate of premature children is still quite high and you know that premature children (i. e., newborns with a birthweight below 3 pounds) are greatly "at risk" to be brain-damaged. The rate of premature children in Nebraska is about 8%, and in Sweden it is about 3%. These figures tell us how much we all still have to do in preventive work as to prenatal and perinatal activities. In observing the number of still-births and infant mortality in our two countries, I will not say there it has to do with more cases, though I would say that early intervention is a fundamental challenge if we plan to continue to lower the number of severely or profoundly retarded citizens in the future. For example, in Sweden, over 90% of the newborn are examined by a pediatrician in the first 5 days of their life. Similarly, after the diagnosis of mental retardation has been confirmed, we really try to take care of these children in a very active way. A few of them can be actively treated and give quite outstanding results, while all of the others can be started on an early habilitation program. But it is not only these activities in the first months which are of importance, it is also vital to put the treatment personnel and the parents on the right track and give them the right attitude about what can be done for these children and how we can activate them. For example, the early activation which many of them need is to start the practice that they are taken out of their beds daily and given a chance to participate in developmentally activating programs, social activities, etc. If you do so, you will find that most of the profoundly-severely retarded can be activated so that they can function as less mentally retarded and less dependent in later life.

Let me take one example. I spoke about premature children, and about 15 years ago there was accomplished a very thorough follow-up on a large group of premature children in England. As you know English pediatricians are very famous -- especially for their work in Child Neurology. They found that 60% of their premature children were mentally handicapped and/or mentally retarded. They actively worked more and more with this group of premature children and the number of handicapped has decreased to 13% from the initial 60% noted 15 years earlier! Interestingly, of this 13%, only 7% were distinctly abnormal, and 6% were called doubtful. Still, if we say that 13% of premature children are mentally delayed, this figure tells us that if we are active with these "at risk" children and give them a greater chance to develop, then all future handicapped children -- not only just the mentally retarded -- will be pushed developmentally upwards so that many go out of the range of mental retardation and up to the range of what you call a slow learner. Similarly, some specific symptoms which we find in brain injured children will be pushed up to the range of normal functioning and they won't come out as handicapped children. I wanted to give you these figures, since I feel that it is very urgent to promote more preventive activities and attitudes from professionals and all treatment personnel. An interesting sidelight is that we have made dramatic advances in preventive medicine as to infectious diseases, so that now very few children are hospitalized for that reason -- and now professionals do have the time to pay more interest to the severe and profoundly retarded children.

I will give you another example of what we find is urgent to do with small children. We did a screening of all our 30,000 mentally retarded children, young adults and adults to see how many were blind, or had some degree of blindness and/or deafness. We found that 3% of our mentally retarded were blind and half as many (i. e., 1.5%)were deaf. It was a combined total of 500 persons. We found to our surprise that there were also 150 who were both blind and deaf. Among the latter group there are surely many that were not mentally retarded, but they were tabulated as such. Now first of all, we were surprised that we had so many blind, and we looked at the rate in the normal population. As you know, it is very difficult to find such figures on normals, but we know how many we have in the school age who are blind, deaf or both. We found that the number of non-mentally retarded children who are blind are very few -- being only a third of those who are deaf. There are two times as many deaf "normal" children as there are blind children in the non-retarded population -- while among the population of the retarded this relationship is reversed. This indicated to us that there might be a possible correlation between blindness and mental retardation in children. Then we did a screening of how this particular double handicap (i. e. blind-retarded, or deaf-retarded) was related to the level of mental retardation. We noted that the deaf mentally retarded were distributed in frequency about the same as others who were not mentally retarded. They were fairly well distributed among the range of levels of the retarded (i. e. , not an increased percentage in any particular level of mental retardation). However, the blind-mentally retarded were distributed downward so there were relatively more who were profoundly retarded than there were those who were moderately retarded. Further, we noted that many of these blind-mentally retarded children had many specific symptoms which we earlier thought were secondary to their blindness. You know, we often speak about special symptoms which we think are part of a disease state, and many of these particular children are very introverted and autistic and never display much direct contact with reality or with persons around them. In studying how small children are developmentally stimulated and how they grasp reality during the first months, you may know that the main source of stimulation for babies is through skin stimulation (i. e. , tactile). After the first month, increasing stimulation comes through vision and later (nine to 12 months of age) comes stimulation through hearing, and then visual and motor perceptive. That is, they think in pictures and it leads to thinking in words which they initially have taken up through hearing. Now you can understand that if a child is blind he runs a serious risk wherein he may not be stimulated at all. Also the stimulation response from the skin tends to increase at age two to three months, and stimulation through hearing remains crucial. Hence, it is important to note that in the first 12 months of life, the child is in a vacuum: nothing "tells" the child anything, and the child can become introverted since he has nothing to think about and nothing to tell, and he just goes inward. He may never grasp reality, or what happens around him, and most of these children stay in this situation and the parents -- who are often unable to stimulate such a child -- become depressed over the situation, and may slowly disengage themselves from their child. This is only one example of how urgent it is to do early case finding, so that we can direct our child psychologist that in this situation he must do everything to find new pathways into the child and that it is really crucial to try to get the child out of the autistic encasement or he will stay developmentally regressed for the rest of his life.

I will now speak a little about those retarded individuals which we all have so many of in our countries and we really must improve our treatment approaches for them. It is very common in Europe, and in this country, to organize special wards for intensive self-help skill(s) training of the severe-profoundly retarded adults.

It is common to note programs which stress personnel and treatment aids. However, most of these special wards are wrong on one major point: they contain too many patients. In my opinion, "too many" is over six patients. Even if they have many personnel and elaborate treatment aids, you will still miss the point that the major program ingredient is not to have more personnel working with the profoundly severe mentally retarded children or adults. Instead, you must structure the environment so that the severe-profoundly retarded person can be dressed and helped to understand something of what happens around him. Otherwise, there are no directional changes in these adults as to their developmental growth. For example, one of our earliest studies was with a group of six adult men who had always soiled themselves and were behaviorally overactive. We established a specific program for them and had some special arrangements for them. When these retarded adults could help themselves, we also noted that it relieved a lot of work for the personnel and they loved it! We found a lot of other things, such as when we measured the weight of the laundry used by the retarded adults who had been specially trained in self-help skills. For example, we weighed the laundry used for the first ten days of the two months of training and we compared this with the last 10 days of these two months. We found that as their behavior improved -- we saved many dollars since they needed much less laundry. Now these are the figures and facts which impress greatly the politicals, since it is a language which helps explain what we are describing to them when we say that these retarded men behaved better. For example, we found that for the first 10 day period of these two months, these six patients had to have their dirty shirts changed 60 times; compared with 39 times during the last 10 days. Similarly, the personnel had to change these six men's pants 84 times during the first ten days and only 26 times the last 10 days; they had to clean the floor 143 times the first 10 days, and 67 times the last. Bedclothes and sheets were changed 77 times against 26 in the two periods. We saved a lot, since these materials and/or work activities were reduced about 40% overall -- and we were doing nothing special! The patients were not specially trained and they were not closely observed and they were not prevented from acting out. The major factor was that they got more attention in a smaller environment -- where they could explore dressing. It was easier for them to find out what they could do and as they seemed to understand reality more clearly, they became more activated in directions of self-care and self-control.

So we noted that the benefits of a smaller environment for these six men could be measured -- as we saved about 4 pounds of laundry a day; we also saved money, and the patients "saved-learned" much more! If you view the results of this approach to these groups of men for 10 to 20 years, as we have done in Sweden, you will understand that it is best to build small units, since the capital cost is very small compared with all of the money wasted on extra laundry, furniture destruction, and the low-level of the patient's behavior in the long run. This is one example of the type of "hard data" which is needed to change our approaches and expectations in managing the severely retarded and the entire trend can be viewed as all-of-one piece.

Now at one of our hospitals we also have had for many years a ward for intensive training. It is specially arranged for 4 or 5 profoundly retarded and most of them stay there for six months. This ward is arranged so that they eat in their own dining room, have their daily training lessons there, and they stay on this ward as much as possible. The personnel are also together with them the whole day. There is naturally something like behavior modification within it, but it is nothing like the type of the behavior modification like you have in this country -- none of the piles of writing day-by-day. Instead, it is primarily based on intense personal contact, an attitude of love between the personnel, the rich physical environment as to color, in the new furniture of the latest styles which you can find, and a really rich normal environment. Now we have done these ward programs for some years and our psychologists have followed-up and they can show that these adult mentally retarded behave themselves more independently and better in all dimensions. However, the most interesting result of the follow-up study was that when these intensively trained adults moved from this special intensive ward back to their old ward (which most often was a ward with 24 to 30 persons), they deteriorated in practically every aspect and at every point! Indeed, they deteriorated all the way back to where they were before they entered the special ward. For example, their social behavior -- which had dramatically improved during their one year stay on the special ward became very primitive again. From this type of follow-up experiences, we can truly appreciate how reflective the environment is to the retarded person as to expected behavior. Therefore, it is not enough to start an intensive training program or to start training programs in a new setting, if you plan afterwards to move them back to the old ward -- since this move cannot keep them on the highest possible level of functioning.

We have also found that when you move over to the new wards

(i. e. , new wards with small groups of 6 to 10 profoundly retarded),
that these groups should be very heterogeneous -- so that they
all are not functioning at a low level. Instead, we try to organize
ward populations where there are always some who are more active or more outgoing, and only one or two in the ward who are
very profoundly retarded or wheel-chaired. We call this heterogeneous grouping instead of homogeneous grouping, since the
latter is the old medical model. The medical model implied that
all who have the same needs and the same diagnosis should be on
the same ward since they surely have the same habits or needs.
We have organized our groups on a heterogeneous basis and find
that this is a very stimulating group organization for the most
severe-profoundly retarded ones. And more than that -- it is
also more stimulating for the personnel, since they can get some
feedback for their efforts from some of their patients and don't
get worn out so easily by those very profoundly retarded who
cannot give them much personal feedback for their efforts. Since
these heterogeneous wards are more active, the personnel love
to be there and they don't complain as they did earlier that the
work is "so difficult" and the patients "so hopeless". We have
noted that the whole atmosphere changes when we utilize these
heterogeneous groupings.

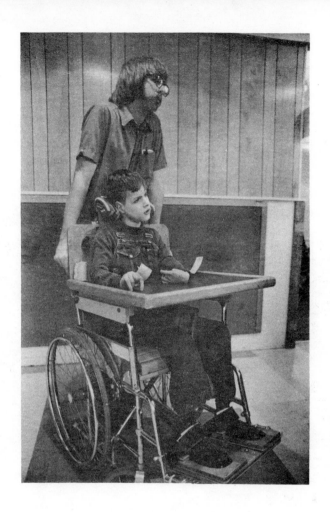

The positioning chair is a relatively recent innovation in the treatment of multiply-handicapped, non-ambulatory persons. Its purpose is to stabilize the handicapped person in an upright position. From this vantage point, the person is immediately more aware of other people and of his environment, and more suitably positioned for the learning of feeding and self-help skills. The positioning chair, which must be individually fitted to the person, can be equipped with neck, hand, and foot stabilizers; these are helpful in diminishing spastic movements and the abnormal neck reflex often found in severely retarded persons who have associated multiple handicaps.

A vivid contrast to drab and depressing institutional settings is the Developmental Maximation Unit of ENCOR in Omaha, Nebraska. Bright colors, attractive and comfortable furniture, and a happy decor are a developmental stimulus in themselves to the handicapped person, and are a normalizing influence in his transition to the outside world. A normal and attractive setting is also important in maintaining the enthusiasm and morale of the unit's staff.

Love is an ingredient quite beyond the planning or measurement of a developmental program. For the severely handicapped child, who has often been rejected and unloved, warm affection can nourish growth that would otherwise never take place. Love awakens an awareness of self and others, provokes and rewards imitation, and supports the child in new learning situations. Significantly, a number of the teachers at ENCOR's DMU are mothers with families of their own.

We have arranged, during the last 10 years, a new special
hospital in Sweden for 100 multiply handicapped retarded who we
transferred from an old hospital. These patients used to be called
"custodial" and many were bedridden or wheelchaired. We started
this hospital because though other children and young adults who
were equally handicapped were viewed as candidates for active
help from the point of view of their need for physical activation --
hospital people tend to be particularly hostile to these same handicaps when they are present in a retarded person! In the past, we
had to train both the patients and the whole hospital staff before
we could take care of the mentally retarded, and because this is
difficult -- there was no hospital in Sweden which was especially
designed and/or programmed for the handicapped severe-p·ofoundly
mentally retarded. Though some hospitals would take "custodial"
cases, no one could tell us what to do if we planned to activate
these children and adults. So we said, "We will do it ourselves,"
and then we built two of these hospitals, and ove the years we
have treated the physically disabled mentally reta·ded there for
an average of six months. They were there for special operations
(i. e. , orthopedic) and general psycho-social activation, then
moved back to their private homes or to their residential homes.

We have learned so much during these last 10 years that we now know that we no longer need these special hospitals, since we have now finally taken care of the group of neglected cases from the past, and new ones are now examined very early, and we now get the orthopedics services at different general hospitals, and start doing the activation procedures elsewhere. This is one example of how we can change a pattern of service from highly specialized to less specialized by showing what can be done and then how to do it elsewhere without building new hospitals all the time!

Another trend is what we do with our deaf and/or blind mentally retarded adults. You know, handicapped children always seem to get into special schools since there is much public interest around children, but there are very few of the general public who have any prolonged interest in the adult retarded -- especially the blind and/or deaf ones. We have one special residential home with about 100 adult mentally retarded-blind where we started special training in personal habits. To our astonishment we found this particular residential home was so successful -- not only in teaching these adults to understand the world around them more fully and behave more independently -- that the Directoress reported to me that she had taught many of them to, "Not be blind anymore !" When I heard this statement, I said to myself that it

must be one of those "lies" which all optimistic people must have,

so I went down to take a personal look at the Directoress' claim.

She showed me many patients who, when she started to show them

pictures and ask where they could find things like a tree, or she

would simply ask, "What is this?" -- the patients would first feel

the card (since they had been taught to do that elsewhere) and he

could not feel anything. Then the Directoress would say, "Take

away your fingers", and "What do you see?", and many would say

"There is something there". They could see the difference between

black and white, and she trained these people and told them that

what they saw on the card was, for example, a tree, and what you

see there is a house, etc. The patients then started to look more

and more at the pictures and label what they did see, and after a

half-year of training these persons could see, and they could under-

stand what they were seeing. Indeed, these were persons that

were, as a matter of fact, made blind by us. They were diagnosed

as blind children once, and put into a school for the blind, and

shouldn't you actually be blind if you are in one of those schools?

So as they were taught via techniques for the blind, they were

also taught to "behave" as the blind and they had not been taught

to understand what they still could see. There really are very

38

few totally blind people -- especially children -- in our world.
However, if you don't see very well and you are also retarded --
then being put into a school for the blind does not allow you to
learn or utilize what you can see! I have never experienced a
clearer example of the difference between vision and perception.
This is a wonderful example that retarded people can also forget
to perceive and/or understand what they still can "see" or observe. They no longer are interested in what they can see --
for they are not taught to understand what they can see and soon
they behave in the manner of the blind. This is only one example
of what happens with so many of our profoundly retarded in our
institutions. We impose upon them to behave as more mentally
retarded than they really are.

We are all well-trained as experts or personnel who help
mentally retarded persons and to diagnose everything that is abnormal -- and we are very interested in the abnormal and im-
pressed with our ability to diagnose same. We are less interested in understanding what is still normal in these persons. We
seem to have more concern with what they cannot do, than in
what they can do! Therefore, I am hesitant to hire personnel --
especially the physicians and psychiatrists -- who are so very
well-trained in diagnosing very small abnormalities in people's

behaviors, since these small signs so often become big things which at once are put on the patient's head as a firm diagnosis for the rest of this person's life. Then the patient is categorized, and both parents are often told that there is nothing that can be done with a person who has this diagnosis. Therefore, we must admit that the most neglected part of this whole matter of treatment for the severe and profoundly retarded rests on our attitude. It is we who must understand our biases, and we who must change in our ways of using our knowledge and our negative attitudes. Sometimes I say in Sweden that it would be better to hire un-trained personnel to take care of our severe-profoundly retarded. I am interested in well-trained personnel if they are still dedicated to their work, and are dedicated to transforming normal behavioral settings so that they can help on what can still be accomplished. Most importantly, they must be interested in how to introduce and fully utilize methods, normal attitudes, and normal relations. For example, I have spoken to many well-trained people who continually say that severe and profoundly retarded children and adults don't understand and cannot speak -- therefore, you do not need to speak with them, or talk to them such as when washing their faces, etc. Yet I find many, many optimistic persons who come from the outside (i. e., not trained) who speak to severe-profoundly retarded children as they have always done with their own children, and when they wash them they do it in a loving fashion as they take the towel and coo to them, coax them, etc. This type of normal stimulation is the crucial matrix of external-internal perceptual stimulation -- a dimension which is a fundamental basis for all developmental approaches to our severe-profoundly retarded children. Therefore, I think that we have so much to learn from people coming from the outside -- not just from the professionals -- and all people can join in to actually help start the new human-scale environments for all of our severe and profoundly retarded patients -- not only just for the mildly and moderately retarded ones as we have so often done up to this time. Indeed, our changing attitudes of new hope and services for the severe and profoundly retarded will permit us to _fully_ utilize the international trends that I have reviewed.

REFERENCES

Grunewald, K. The guiding environment: The dynamics of residential living. Washington, D.C.: U.S. Department of Health, Education and Welfare, 1972.

Grunewald, K. A rural county in Sweden: Malmöhus county. In R. B. Kugel and W. Wolfensberger (Eds.), Changing patterns in residential services for the mentally retarded. Washington D.C.: The President's Committee on Mental Retardation.

THE CROSS DISCIPLINARY-CROSS MODALITY APPROACH TO SERVICES FOR THE DEVELOPMENTALLY DISABLED WHO HAVE PHYSICAL HANDICAPS

Introduction (Paul Pearson)

Mrs. Haynes is the Associate Director and Nurse Consultant for the Professional Services Program Department of the United Cerebral Palsy Associations, Inc. She is the author of *A Developmental Approach to Casefinding,* one of the most popular monographs ever published by the U.S. Public Health Service and she also edited the American version of Nancie Finnie's book titled, *Handling the Young Cerebral Palsied Child at Home.*

I know of no one who has brought a greater personal commitment to their work. Una has devoted a professional lifetime to improving the services of those handicapped by cerebral palsy. While her concerns are for all the handicapped, her heart lies with the "babies." I believe it was this basic concern as much as anything which led her to develop the programs which she is about to describe for us. She, probably as much as anyone in this country, is actively meeting Dr. Grunewald's challenging statement that much of the behavior currently found among the severely and profoundly retarded is *not* characteristic of their "retardedness," but rather is the raw consequence of lack of programs.

It is with real pleasure that I present this charming lady and my good friend, Una Haynes.

THE CROSS DISCIPLINARY-CROSS MODALITY APPROACH TO SERVICES FOR THE DEVELOPMENTALLY DISABLED WHO HAVE PHYSICAL HANDICAPS
Una Haynes

How many of you envy me trying to follow Dr. Grunewald's most scholarly presentation? Let me say that he has described the problems more succinctly and accurately than ever I could. He has also objectively stated that his countrymen faced the same problems a few years ago which now challenge us, so he truly understands our situation. While we may be ashamed to admit the inadequacy of service which now obtains in the United States, it is important that we do so as a foundation to effect positive change.

We might well focus our discussions together today upon the needs to expand and improve programs of primary prevention; the need to improve the basic health of parents of tomorrow and promote the birth of healthy babies. We could also focus upon present approaches and the continuing need to expand programs for earlier detection of anomaly and dysfunction among our new-borns. However, I have been asked to share with you today some comments about two ongoing programs initiated by UCPA. One of these is a collaborative effort which has obtained the continued endorsement of the National Association for Retarded Children and the support of the Division of Developmental Disabilities in the Department of Health, Education, and Welfare. Together we sought to improve the lot of residents in state institutions who had extensive neuromotor and neurosensory disabilities in addition to significant mental retardation. In essence this project focused upon "the least of these..." in an effort to enrich the lives of individuals who have many unwarranted secondary disabilities due to lack of early recognition, immediate and/or sustained provision of comprehensive services. The other project is focused upon disabled babies under two years of age, an effort to help prevent such unwarranted secondary disabilities and to enable these babies to achieve their ultimate potential for development in cognitive, social and emotional as well as physical aspects of habilitation. Hopefully, in future years, we will be able to report, in triumph, major advances in primary prevention of disabilities.

I. Purpose and Priority of the Project.

Advances in medical science are contributing to the survival of severely damaged infants and appear to be increasing the longevity of individuals who have significant neuromotor and neurosensory handicaps, in addition to serious and profound mental retardation. The nature of the developmental needs and the personal care problems of such individuals presents a unique challenge for parents and the professions involved, as well as for the individuals who must cope with these multiple disabilities. There are both ethical and economic bases to support the application of special approaches to aid these individuals. For some, it could mean the ability to function in the community; for others, an early return to the community from a residential institution; for the longer-term residents, an improved level of health, greater functional independence and mobility, which will facilitate their participation in a broader range of residential programs.

The primary objectives of the project were focused on the need to assist mentally retarded individuals with severe and multiple neuromotor and neurosensory disabilities, to attain their optimum potential for habilitation. Time does not permit a comprehensive review of all factors involved in the planning and implementation of this project, however, many of those present today have already participated in a workshop on this project or had other opportunities to hear about it. Therefore, only a few highlights will be reviewed.

Ideally, both community and residential facilities should employ, in adequate numbers, staff members highly skilled in the entire rubric of habilitation and life enrichment services. Facilities and equipment should be designed to foster the achievement of these goals. Instead, the very architecture of facilities

46

and particularly residential institutions, with rows and rows of beds, serious overcrowding, lack of program space, lack of appropriate equipment, and assignment of the least well prepared aids and attendants to serve the multi-handicapped, were found to be the rule, rather than the exception, in many U.S. facilities. In a few residential centers, a token approach to rehabilitation was found where there had been provided one very expensively equipped "therapy room" (often filled with equipment better suited to the arthritic and post-traumatic patients rather than the devel - opmentally disabled). One physical therapist may be employed to render service in a facility where there are several hundred res- idents with severe physical as well as other disabilities. A few residents may be taken to this room for direct service by a ther- apist, while the others continue to become increasingly disabled while lying in their beds or placed in similarly horizontal and immobile positions on the floor, for part of each day.

In an heroic effort to share their skills and competencies to serve more residents, some of the physical, occupational and speech therapists in residential centers each trained some "ther- apy aides". Fanning out to the wards, these aides were noted to exercise the residents a few moments, to try to provide hand function activity and/or some language development for a short period. By carrying out such activities once a day, a few times a week or per month, it was hoped to demonstrate positive gains among additional residents. However, the key aides assigned to the 24-hour care of such residents (in essence their parent surrogates) did not usually see this role in total habilitation effort nor were they taught or motivated to carry out a functional integration of therapeutic goals throughout their normal interactions with the residents during the rest of the day and night. Often they resented the fact that another aide would "interrupt" the ward routine for these few moments "doing things" to the residents that their parent-surrogates neither understood not accepted as being of value.

Due to the severity of handicaps, supervision of these units was often assigned to registered nurses. Here again, there was often lack of communication, contact, or collaborative effort between the "rehabilitation specialists" and the nursing personnel. It may not be wise to cite a few points like these without referring to the whole spectrum of collaborative effort to habilitation which is needed to effect positive change. For instance, the measures needed to obtain appropriate cooperation from the dietary department including foods of different textures, time to introduce and carry out better feeding techniques, measures to foster self-feeding and dining areas separate from the bed space. Measures to persuade cottage life personnel that the severely handicapped can indeed benefit from recreational and other life enrichment services and a variety of truly educational advances, when positioned to foster visual and auditory attending behaviors, eye-hand coordination, etc., are also greatly needed, before the severely disabled can move out of the segregated minimal life support milieu of custodial wards into the mainstream of programming provided for other residents. These are but a few of the broad range of collaborative efforts required to effect positive change.

By means of grants of $2,500 each from United Cerebral Palsy Associations, Inc., the Mental Retardation Division and the National Association for Retarded Children, plus the cooperation of the staff at the Central Wisconsin Colony and Training School, a new curriculum concept and bibliography were developed which incorporated new and innovative ideas and techniques for providing improved services for such individuals and their families. Slides, films and a variety of improvised equipment items were developed.

Following the selection of the five institutions which would collaborate on this project, five teams were to be prepared by means of the new curriculum. Because the target population had such severe physical as well as other handicaps, the first teams were made up of therapists and nurses who would render immediate support and assistance to the care-contact staff. By working very closely with educators, psychologists and others in cottage life as well as medical staff, it was hoped these teams would help to achieve a marriage between the so-called medical and educational approaches to service. The generic aide group, serving as 24-hour parent surrogates, would be helped to increase their knowledge and skills in creating and carrying out a therapeutic regime in a therapeutic environment (the term "therapeutic" being defined by this project as a milieu designed to foster social, emotional and intellectual, as well as physical development). Additionally, the teams would have an advocacy role on behalf of the residents and their parent surrogates with other personnel and divisions of the total service complex of the institution.

While the project would originate in institutional settings there would be constant study of the applications of the findings to community-based environments, rendering service to individuals and to their own family members, either in their own homes, community day care or smaller community residential facilities.

An underlying need was to delineate the measures which would help team personnel to share and extend their knowledge and skills with others in new and more effective ways; to see if the teams could both support and enhance the knowledge and skills of the care-contact staff (the "aide-mothers and fathers") and foster the achievement of the primary goal to effect positive change in a target group so handicapped that they had previously been deemed unable to benefit from anything more than custodial care. Superintendents of the collaborating institutions would be expected to agree to support the project goals, help create smaller, family-type groups of individuals to whom the aides could relate more directly and consistently. There were no funds to increase the staff complement nor to effect the architectural changes which were needed so desperately to overcome the dehumanizing environment of the large wards but small grants were available to permit the purchase and appropriate adaptations of special equipment, documenting the changes in the residents and similar aspects of project activities. The following objectives were delineated for the teams to be trained:

1. To acquire through interdisciplinary action, appropriate attitudes and skills which aid in the assessment and

developmental management of the individual who has neuromotor and related neurosensory problems;

2. To gain ability in the observation and assessment of the status of the individual in relation to organic and environmental factors as they influence his ability to meet his daily needs;

3. To develop the ability to contribute effectively to the development of a comprehensive plan to meet the needs of the individual;

4. To acquire additional skill in applying techniques necessary in implementing the individualized program;

5. To focus on methods and materials useful in transmitting this knowledge and skill to parents, parent surrogates and other personnel concerned with the individual's improvement.

An additional grant from the Division of Mental Retardation (now Division of Developmental Disabilities) in April 1970, matched by UCPA funds was utilized to support this project. The five collaborating institutions were then selected and prepared by means of the new curriculum. Each team was made up of a nurse responsible for inservice education, a nurse with significant responsibility for nursing practice, a registered occupational therapist and a registered physical therapist.

a. From July 15 to August 15, 1970, an intensive course of instruction with a strong component of clinical practice was conducted at Central Wisconsin Colony under the direction of Mrs. Dorothy Hutchinson, Associate Professor, Specialist in Continuing Education, University of Wisconsin. Mrs. Hutchinson and seven faculty members maintained close liaison with the teams and there were two site visits made to each facility during the first year.

b. In June 1970, the teams and faculty reconvened. The keen interest and support of the administrators and medical advisors, the interaction of teams with other personnel in the fields of nutrition, education and recreation as well as significant, positive change in the target population and their parent surrogates led to a request for project continuation. Marked interest in the project evidenced by a variety of university and other personnel also promoted interest in mounting a conference on the project.

c. In June 1971, the award of a supplemental grant by the Division of Developmental Disabilities made it possible both to continue testing these approaches and mount a conference which was held during the Annual meeting of the American Association on Mental Deficiency in Minneapolis, Minnesota, in May, 1972.

Mrs. Hutchinson and seven members of the faculty have now spent a total of 58 days in sequential site visits over a period of 24 months to each of the five participating teams in the five collaborating agencies.

They have been continuously monitoring the adequacy of the original curriculum, supplementing, modifying and extending certain parameters of instruction, based on interactions with the target population, team members and team colleagues. All of these pertiment factors are now being incorporated in revised curriculum guidelines for use by university, college and other personnel interested in training new teams.

1. To provide a re-definition of the philosophy and rationale for the cross-disciplinary, cross-modality approach which evolved in the course of the project (these will be discussed later in greater detail).

2. To review the problems encountered and how they were met, both in preparing the teams and in the implementation of the program in the five collaborating facilities.

3. To discuss the relevance of this approach when applied to a less severely but similarly involved target group of multi-handicapped individuals and their parents or parent surrogates (a ripple effect).

4. To review team activities in cooperation with agencies other than their own and the potential for applying the findings from this project to a variety of community as well as residential facilities.

III. The Nationally Organized Collaborative Infant Project

The second collaborative project initiated by UCPA in September 1971, first involved a consortium of five diverse collaborating centers, all serving babies under 2 years of age who evidenced developmental delays or developmental aberration. These ongoing centers agreed to share all their experience, knowledge and skills and collaborate on the distillation of exemplary components of services for the babies and their families.

As Dr. Grunewald has pointed out, if we are "active" with these children, especially with the babies, we can hopefully push them upward developmentally. Perhaps it may be relevant to discuss, briefly, some of the rationale underlying this project.

54

tant for the normal child, may be more crucial for the infant with a physical disability". Unfortunately, there is some evidence that the type and degree of attention focused on remediation or alleviation of a physical disability tends to obscure other equally important aspects of programing for a child with multiple handicaps. These include cognitive, social and emotional aspects of development, and due attention to the critical importance of the "attachment" behaviors between mother and child. Bowlby points out that attachment (and attachment behavior) develops as a consequence of proximity and reciprocal interaction. He maintains that the infant has a bias towards attachment to a single figure, usually the mother or parent surrogate but that attachments can develop to other persons. The nature of other attachments that may develop will both affect the attachment to the mother and the role of the mother in relation to her child. As a consequence, if a substantial proportion of the child's waking time is spent outside the home in a therapy center receiving treatment from the therapists to alleviate a physical disability, the mother-child relationship will be affected quite extensively. Even if a planned program is carried out primarily in the home by the parents, it will alter in some way the interaction between parent and child. Since this relationship is a basic factor in child development, it is important to consider carefully, evaluate critically and control effectively the impact of any given therapeutic regimen on the infant's total development and the parent-child relationship as well as its effectiveness relative to his physical problem.

Personnel from consortium centers, also working with older children, recognized the critical importance of viewing the total impact of orthopedic procedures or therapy programs which are directed to the physical problem among this group. For instance, if elective surgery for remediation of an orthopedic defect is the medical approach of choice at a given stage in the child's life, the timing, as well as the nature of this intervention must be planned with care. Traditionally, the care exercised has often been focused primarily on the availability of a skilled orthopedist, the contingencies of the operating room schedule and the availability of hospital bed space. These are important factors and certainly worthy of attention. However, if the date selected in this manner also requires that the child will miss school at a very critical period of instruction or means that the child will return home to find his mother preoccupied with a new baby who has "taken his place" during his surgical stay, these and similar factors must also be carefully weighed. It seems hardly necessary to point out that when one considers the total spectrum of development, rather than the physical disability in isolation, such factors may well deserve at least equal or much greater attention than the fortuitous juxtaposition of surgical schedules and available hospital beds.

No individual with a physical handicap should be denied the full mobilization of all areas of expertise which can be brought to bear on his behalf. The question at issue is the need to use this expertise most effectively, integrate the parameters of service related to the physical disability with a positive rather than deleterious effect upon the other aspects of the child's total development and do so within the rubric of the family's own life style.

The traditional model of the interdisciplinary team approach to service for individuals with multiple disabilities has usually included one or more representative from several medical disciplines, physical, occupational and speech therapy, nursing, social work, psychology, education, etc. It is customary for all team members to participate in the diagnostic and evaluation process. Thereafter, in the presence of a physical disability, the individual is frequently assigned to receive treatment several times a day, week or month by qualified physical, occupational and/or speech therapists. While there are exceptions, the usual pattern of service delivery has been for each therapist to schedule treatments on a one-to-one basis with the child, or assign a trained aide to carry this out under her surveillance. This has often resulted in withdrawing the child from his classroom or developmental group one or more periods of time daily or weekly to "go to therapy", requiring him to miss much valuable instruction. Another alternative has been to require the child to go to a separate therapy center or room after school, giving him long days of "all work and no play". Additionally, lists of exercises were given to parents for them to carry out at home. Faithful adherence to these exercise patterns not only increase the child's "work day" but also affect the parent-child relationships and the family's life style. In dealing with handicapped adults, the situation is somewhat different. However, in programs dealing with children, this classical model of interdisciplinary care has tended (with some exceptions) to surround a disabled child with authoritarian figures, each doing something to one or more parts of his body, doing so with some frequency to help alleviate or remediate his physical disability and involving the family to give exercise in a structured way without much prior evaluation of the family's own life style.

This pattern of service also reduced the number of individuals one therapist could serve. Even when the therapist worked with small groups part of the time instead of on a consistent one-to-one relationship with each child, long waiting lists developed in many therapy centers.

In recent years heightened interest in early casefinding has increased referral of very young infants with physical and other disabilities who cannot tolerate excessive or inconsistent handling by a variety of adults. In addition to the important consideration of attachment behaviors and early learning, these factors caused many thoughtful physicians, therapists, nurses and others who had a sound background in growth and development, to carefully re-assess their respective and traditional "interdisciplinary" roles on behalf of the disabled infant and his family.

Sharing these interests and concerns, United Cerebral Palsy Associations, Inc. initiated the "Nationally Organized Collaborative Infant Project" with the help of a grant from the Bureau of Education for the Handicapped. As previously mentioned, this project involves a consortium of five centers with ongoing diverse programs. A few slides have been selected to provide an overview of some of the components in these programs.

All centers involved share in common the provision of comprehensive inter-disciplinary diagnostic and evaluation services, repeated at appropriate intervals. All centers view the parents as primary programmers for these infants. Each center differs somewhat in the delivery of service on an ongoing basis. Every infant and family is provided with the full spectrum of expertise available through the highly skilled professional staff members but this service is provided in new ways. I will now illustrate some examples of the way programs may be designed and carried out, focusing particularly on the cross-disciplinary and cross-modality approach utilized in the implementation of the service program.

It is well known that long before a normal infant can use his hand effectively he brings it to his visual horizons, regards it intensely and evidences awareness of it as it moves in space. Let us consider an infant who may have evidenced a paucity of movement on the left side. While he could move the left arm and hand he did not tend to do so. One activity a mother can be encouraged to carry out, as part of her normal nurturing of the baby, is to place a mobile first on his right side. The slightest touch makes it bob about. The bright colors attract him visually, a bell tinkles

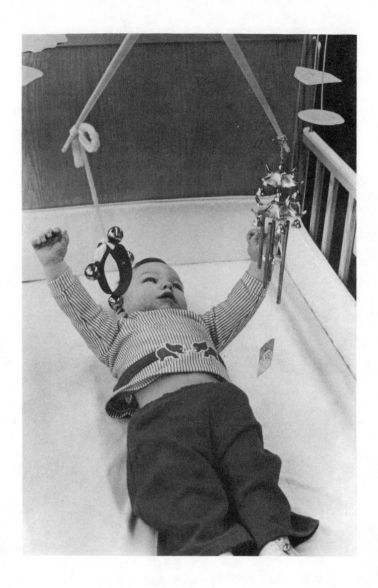

A mobile is an extremely good toy to have by the child's bedside. It provides simultaneous tactile, visual, and auditory stimuli, and can aid the development of the normal or the retarded child.   Here, the crib-bound child uses his less-developed left hand to reach for the mobile.

Like the mobile, the "busy box" is an excellent developmental toy; it is particularly useful for refining the child's manual skills. In this photograph, the placement of the busy box is important, for it compels the interested child to a standing position.

The interdisciplinary team has the advantage of simultaneous observation and interpretation of the child's behavior. Here the team is composed of an orthopedic specialist, speech therapist, physical therapist, and the mother, who observe and interact with the child.

giving him auditory reinforcement. When he succeeds in grasping
the mobile, it dances up and down. Then the mobile is placed on
his left side motivating its use on the affected side. The mother
can do the ironing or be otherwise involved in meeting other
family needs (i. e., preparing a family meal). Later, the same
baby can be surrounded by a variety of equipment.

As the baby develops, it is important that he be exposed to
many different types of textures, different types of sounds, toys
which have motion, a flashlight perhaps, which could help him to
identify the source of light, or which may be used to focus on different parts of his body, to bring them to his attention. In other
words, there is a carefully prescribed program of the appropriate
visual, auditory, motor and other stimuli which may be pertinent
in fostering his development.

Let us see how staff can work together to suggest ways which
foster several parameters of infant development. Perhaps the
teacher has suggested the "busy box" as a learning experience,
the occupational therapist because it motivates good hand function,
and the physical therapist because a change of placement can
motivate the baby to come to standing.

The "busy box" is simply a toy panel which offers to the baby
a telephone dial, bells and clangers, sliding devices and spinners,

all of which help to develop his visual, auditory and manual skills. By use of such a toy the baby is being motivated to achieve therapeutic goals without direct handling. The fact that the teacher and two therapists can work out the program together is one example of cross-disciplinary programming helping the baby. Each team member is working toward the attainment of a specific goal but have coordinated these objectives in this single activity. This is also but one example out of many others wherein the mother's "normal" interaction with the child and providing experiences which do not necessarily require her entire attention are oriented to achieve a therapeutic goal in a way that is part of the family's own life style.

An important aspect of the cross-disciplinary approach is the concept of the parents as primary programmers.

All professional members of the team will be involved with the child's evaluation. The therapists, physicians, educators and others on the team will have tried out different approaches to foster attainment of developmental goals and considered together how these might be included into a reasonably integrated program suitable for an infant of this age and with these problems. The public health nurse on the team will not only provide her own expertise related to basic health and other needs but also visit in the home, studying the family's own life style, helping to evaluate the program plan in its relationship to other family interests and needs. The parents' own evaluation of the child and their goals for him must be an integral part of the planning process. During these early months of life the normal attachment behavior of child to close family members is reinforced. Often the parents and the public health nurse develop a warm relationship during the first months of the baby's life and this may lead to the mutual decision of the family and other team members that the health nurse will be the team facilitator. As such, she will help carry out the several parameters of infant service, do so in the home and direct the support of the family until child and family are ready for group programming such as a pre-nursery experience. She visits when the father is home, too. She helps him see and reinforce his baby's abilities. In another case it might be the physical therapist or other member of the team who is the facilitator, in this instance the nurse would share her skills.

The nurse's team colleagues help to instruct her, and she in return helps the family carry out their approaches as well as her own. Her team colleagues have in effect shared their knowledge and skills, released their role to her at this stage in the baby's development but not their accountability for the child's progress in their respective areas of expertise. This release of role to the point of licensure or certification on the part of team members without release of accountability for his maximum progress in their particular area of expertise is the cornerstone of "cross-disciplinary approaches", the term we use to identify this type of service. The team member who serves as team facilitator must also be sensitive to the changing needs of the child and/or parent. For instance, if contractures or related changes in physical function begin to be evident before the next scheduled team evaluation, the nurse will arrange for the orthopedist and/or physical therapist to see the child. If necessary, the baby will be given direct therapy by the specialists. However, direct intervention by all team members is not used unless there is a real need. Emphasis is placed on a broad developmentally oriented habilitation approach, carried on at home and integrated into "normal" family handling and interactions to the greatest possible extent.

When the child and family are ready, the baby is gradually introduced to a pre-nursery group experience. The family and child are now helped to separate from each other for a short period of time.

Again the staff works together to foster the achievement of cognitive, social and emotional as well as physical goals in the total development process. In the pre-nursing experience a number of factors will enhance the "naturalness" of the setting and communications among team members; a lack of uniforms; the presence of family members as well as professional staff; and the non-medical appearance of this milieu where there is a marriage between the so-called "medical" and "educational" approaches to service for the multi-handicapped.

A different approach being used in another consortium center is interdisciplinary evaluation, a specific skills training session for the parents whose home programs are supplemented by these group practice sessions with their babies once or twice a week. The babies in each group have similar potentials and needs, but each child's program has been individualized. The "baby-team" staff members meet before each group session. During the session itself it may be hard to tell which is the speech therapist, the teacher, the social worker, occupational or physical therapist. But they have agreed beforehand on the behavioral goals, the procedures and equipment to be used. For example, while it may be the physical therapist who relates directly to the mother and child, she is immediately encouraging the mother to respond to and reinforce the babbling effort when the babble occurs. In like manner, the speech therapist will also be aware of and reinforce attainment of goals related to the physical therapy aspects of service during her interaction with the parent and child.

While the parents and babies meet with the physicians and other team members in private sessions from time to time, there is also a group meeting on clinic days. The parents are an integral part of the team and are encouraged to play this role, participating in the discussion, the program planning and program implementation for their children. Recognition of and help to implement their role as primary programmers has made parents real members of the habilitation team and established true colleague relations with other team members.

I have talked about cross-disciplinary approaches, and would like to give an example of what is meant by "cross-modality" in the connotations which we apply to this term. One good example was a baby who took one and one-half hours to feed drop by drop because she could not suck or swallow effectively.

Time does not permit the discussion of the detailed evaluations and planning of this child's programs and how other aspects of programming, approved by the physician, were introduced. However, in brief, it was found that research in the field of speech therapy suggested that certain olfactory stimuli, plus cold substances (i. e. , a chilled nipple) might enhance sucking. Brushing and icing of the lips, another "modality" might help her close her lips more effectively (the suggestion of an occupational therapist). A physical therapist, sophisticated in the use of several modalities which might help reduce excessive extensor tone and ways to cope with an asymmetrical tonic neck reflex, suggested a holding position whereby the baby's stiffly extended head and body might be relaxed when her head is placed in the midline, arms placed in front of her and legs flexed.

A nipple created by a German dentist was found to be the one which helped to reduce air leakage around the mouth. The nurse knew that sweet substances enhanced suck so a bit of honey was used on the nipple. A nipple straw was found whereby the baby could draw milk from the base of the bottle (permitting the child to sip milk with the head flexed in the more normal manner). The infant also closed her lips more effectively in this position. Here then are several different modalities, i. e. , a cross-modality approach, each aspect chosen in an eclectic way from the total repertoire which becomes available through the interdisciplinary team. The cross-disciplinary aspects are re-flected in the fact that instead of having five specialists each "doing his own thing" the nurse was the one here designated to put it all together at feeding times and the parents were taught the approach. This particular child was enabled to suck and swallow a full eight-ounce formula in 20 minutes.

Another example is a program which is carried out with a group of less disabled infants in a pre-nursery setting. Even at this early age, the teachers are taught how to integrate and carry out much of the medically related aspects of child's program in the course of his nursery experiences. The therapist and nurse become engaged in team teaching roles. Occasionally, the child may be withdrawn for segregated therapy sessions when indicated but again the emphasis is on promotion of a normative pre-school experience. Of critical importance is the fact that the children are under the surveillance of the highly skilled professional staff members who are constantly monitoring all parameters of progress. Therapists are not segregated in a special room most of the day working on one aspect of a child's program related to his physical function in isolation from team colleagues and from the other aspects of the service program.

To summarize this brief glimpse of a few relevant factors in a major collaborative effort, we should imagine an interdisciplinary team wherein each member holds a key made up of his expertise to try and unlock the door which symbolizes the barriers to development posed by the child's disabilities.

But no one key can successfully turn the lock all the way. However, when each member of the team tries to give the parent or parent surrogate his own special key in his own special way, neither the parent nor the child can cope effectively with this complicated and heavy load.

In the cross-disciplinary approach, each team member pools his expertise to forge one "team key" at a time.

This the parent and child can manage. At other stages of development, new keys will be forged. No single key from any discipline working in isolation can open the door completely for the child with multiple disabilities.

Cross-modality is only possible when each team member is skilled in several approaches (i.e., modalities) and able to select from this repertoire the most suitable measures. A team member must be knowledgeable, skilled and secure in the practice of his or her profession and have sufficient knowledge about a related field to respect a colleague's expertise, before the extensive role release and role sharing involved in the cross-disciplinary approach to the delivery of service can be used successfully by an interdisciplinary team.

There are many other parameters of the project which one might discuss, such as the efforts to document the scientific basis, as well as the empirical judgments of a distinguished group of experts, which underlie various aspects of the program design and implementation. There are many instruments and other measures utilized to assess infant progress, family-centered aspects of evaluation of various program components and the project as a whole. The fact that the collaborating centers are located in different parts of the country, sponsored by different agencies, have differing sources of funds, are monitoring cost effectiveness of various program segments -- are all expected to yield very useful data.

At this time these illustrations from the "baby project" have been used primarily to share some of the common denominators in both endeavors. An expert in the field of adult education has played a very important role in both of these projects. At first glance, one might wonder why a project geared to "infants" and early childhood education, in its broadest sense, would place such importance on adult education. However, the parents and parent surrogates are adults. The physicians, educators, therapists, nurses and other representatives of professions involved in rendering services are adults. Assessing readiness for learning, motivation for learning, methods of teaching and implementation of the teaching-learning process are different for adults than those in teaching children. Team members must teach and learn from each other. Yet sophistication in the field of adult education is not a generic component in the background of most professionals. Both projects focused upon the parents and parent surrogates as key members of the "inter-disciplinary" team. If parents are truly to collaborate in program design and implementation; if team members are to share their knowledge and skills to an optimal degree, the principles of adult education are critical factors in achieving these goals.

I have now seen educators and physicians plus other educationally and medically related personnel sit down together to hammer out goals for a handicapped person, giving equal and simultaneous attention to cognitive, social and emotional, as well as physical, needs. I have seen them state these goals in behavioral terms; delineate the "curriculum", including the materials and procedures to be used; the team members to be involved; where and when the interventions will take place; the projected date when the goals are expected to be met; the evaluative criteria to be used to evaluate goal achievement. Then, follow all this with an analysis as to whether or not the goals were met, an appropriate re-evaluation of all factors involved, and the setting of the next goals.

I have seen parents and parent surrogates supported and assisted to achieve their place on these teams, helping to design the programs as well as directly involved in program implementation. While the strong component of "adult education" cannot be said to be solely responsible for this type of endeavor, it has had a markedly positive influence along these lines in both projects.

In respect to the infants who may still have to cope with some disabilities as they grow older, one would hope that part of their habilitation process will now include both the climate and the ability to function on the teams, able to exert positive influence on program design and having alternative choices available for their consideration in the service delivery system. Without belaboring the point any further, it is suggested that the rubric of adult education within the total spectrum of these projects is worthy of attention by all who share similar interests and concerns, an aspect which may not yet have been given sufficient visibility as we plan together for the future.

Interest and commitment are hard to sustain for long periods of time. The depth and extent of involvement on the part of all concerned with these projects can only be described as worthy of very special commendation.

These are but two out of many endeavors now under way in the United States stemming from out mutual concerns about and interests in the improvement of services for the developmentally disabled and their families. We all recognize the difficulties in attaining the ideal both in providing exemplary service and hopefully the ultimate prevention of many (if not all) of such disabilities in the future.

REFERENCES

Barsch, R. H. Perceptual-motor curriculum. Vol. II. Achieving perceptual-motor efficiency. Seattle: Special Child Publications, 1967.

Bowlby, J. Attachment and loss. Vol. I. Attachment. London: Hogarth, 1969.

Call, J. D. Early identification of children with potential learning problems. In B. K. Keogh (Ed.)., Proceedings of a conference: Early identification of children with potential learning problems, Los Angeles: U. C. L. A., 1969.

Gesell, A. L. & Armatruda, C. S. Development diagnosis: Normal and abnormal child development, clinical methods and pediatric applications. New York: Hoeber, 1947.

Haynes, U. A developmental approach to casefinding. Washington, D. C.: U. S. Department of Health, Education and Welfare, 1967.

Ingram, T. T. A. The new approach to early diagnosis of handicaps in children. Developmental medicine and child neurology 1969, 11, 279-284.

Jones, M. H., Wenner, W. H., Toczek, A. M., & Barrett, M. L. Pre-nursery program for children with cerebral palsy. Journal of American Women's Medical Association, 1962, 17, 713-719.

Kagan, J. Psychological development of the child: Part I. Personality, behavior, and temperament. In F. Falkner (Ed.) Human Development. Philadelphia: W. B. Saunders, 1966.

Kephart, N. C. The slow learner in the classroom. Columbus, Ohio: C. E. Merrill, 1960.

Lipsitt, L. Learning in the human infant. In H. W. Stevenson, E. H. Tess, and H. L. Rheingold (Eds.), Comparative and developmental approaches. New York: Wiley, 1967.

Papousek, H. Conditioning during early postnatal development. In Y. Brackbill and G. S. Thompson (Eds.), Behavior in infancy and early childhood. New York: Free Press, 1967.

Piaget, J. The origins of intelligence in children. (Translated by M. Cook.) New York: International Universities Press, 1952.

Strauss, A. A. & Kephart, N. C. Psychopathy and education of the brain-injured child. Vol. II. Progress in theory and clinic. New York: Grune & Stratton, 1955.

White, B. L. & Held, R. Plasticity of sensory motor development. In J. F. Rosenblith and W. Allinsmith (Eds.), Causes of behavior: Readings in child development and educational psychology (2nd Ed.), Boston: Allyn & Bacon, 1966.

THE SEVERELY-PROFOUNDLY RETARDED AND MULTIPLY HANDICAPPED: COMMUNITY, INSTITUTIONAL, AND UNIVERSITY TRAINING CHALLENGES

Introduction (Frank Menolascino)

The two foregoing presentations have reviewed international trends and techniques for helping the severely and profoundly retarded. Now a panel of experts will discuss challenges which they have noted in the implementation of services for the retarded. Just as our two major speakers have discussed challenges in institutional, community, and home approaches—our panel will also elaborate on these areas of endeavor. The first presentation will be by Charles Galloway, who will discuss the Child Development Services which he directs for the Eastern Nebraska Community Office of Retardation—a regional five-county system of mental retardation services here in Nebraska. His presentation will be followed by two presenters, Ken Keith and Hugh Sage from the Beatrice State Home. The staff of the Beatrice State Home has truly committed itself to redirect its humanistic endeavors of help on behalf of the retarded, and this presentation will address itself to some of the vicissitudes inherent in formulating values, establishing goals, and implementing programmatic objectives for the severely and profoundly retarded within an institutional setting. Dr. Grunewald and Mrs. Haynes have both commented on the crucial dimension of the attitudes and skills of the future cadre(s) of trainees who will work and serve the severely and profoundly retarded. Accordingly, the last member of this panel, Paul Pearson, will focus on how these training challenges are being addressed via the University Affiliated Facility (UAF) approach. The entire UAF thrust in our country holds great promise for providing a systematic nationwide approach to assuring that most vital ingredient of any extended program of help for the severely retarded: well-trained personnel!

GUARANTEEING GROWTH IN THE COMMUNITY: ENCOR's DEVELOPMENTAL PROGRAMS
Charles Galloway

At this time, it seems that our nation is on the verge of a

"paradigm shift" (Kuhn, 1962) with regard to the human manage-

ment of our retarded fellow citizens, both children and adults.

More and more families, professionals, politicians, and social

planners are seriously questioning the mental retardation institu-

tional model that has had a long and checkered history in this

country (e. g. , Wolfensberger, 1969, 1972). The questions center

on issues of both human rights and compatibility with modern

knowledge regarding human development in general. Put simply,

more people are asking whether it is either right or efficacious

to attempt to establish "normal" behavior in abnormal environ-

ments. A large number of court cases are underway to challenge

traditional mental retardation management systems as a result of

landmark court cases related to "right to education" (Pennsylvania

Association for Retarded Children vs the Commonwealth of Penn-

sylvania, 1971) and the provision of treatment involving "least

restraint" (Wyatt vs Stickney, 1971). The momentum of institu-

tional "solutions" to the "problem" of mental retardation is on

the verge of being checked (e. g. , Policy Statement on Residential

Care, National Association for Retarded Children, 1972).

Normalized community-based services for all retarded children have emerged as the paradigmatic alternative to institutional models. Increasingly, communities are investing their human energy and resources in comprehensive local alternatives. Many community mental retardation agencies are being formed to provide these services, but in order to avoid the establishment of "mini-institutions" within town boundaries, these agencies and their confederates must design into their systems means of guaranteeing their clients maximum involvement with the mainstream of the community. These guarantees are particularly critical in the area of early childhood education -- where human development, both delayed and non-delayed, is most plastic.

ENCOR: Foundations and Programs

The Eastern Nebraska Community Office of Retardation (ENCOR) is a five-county regional agency established in 1970 to provide direct and/or indirect services to all retarded citizens within the region. This commitment is made to retarded citizens currently living within the region as well as to those who were placed in the state institution prior to the availability of local alternatives. "Direct" services include developmental-day programs for youngsters, vocational training for adults, and a continuum of residential services for both children and adults.

"Indirect" services comprise such diverse support services as family and client counseling, transportation, developmental evaluation, medical services, recreation, and speech and physical therapy. Through selective combinations of both direct and indirect service types, the likelihood of meeting unique client needs is maximized. At the same time, the agency avoids providing services which an individual does not need or which he can receive from other sources in the community.

The philosophical base of the agency's work is the principle of normalization, which requires the "utilization of means which are as culturally normative as possible, in order to establish and/or maintain personal behaviors and characteristics which are as culturally normative as possible" (Wolfensberger, 1972, p. 28). Four corollaries of the normalization principle should control the design of a community service system for the retarded: dispersal, specialization, integration, and continuity of services (Dybwad, 1969).

I will limit my discussion of these factors primarily to ENCOR's developmental programs for children, although their relevance to other service types is equally applicable. Fig. 1 is a schematic picture of the links between the various ENCOR services.

Unit and the Developmental Centers serve as developmental facilitators which allow children to acquire skills necessary to progress to the Developmental Centers, as well as to other more normalized environments.

Services for retarded citizens should be as integrated into comparable services for the non-retarded population as possible. Integration here includes social and physical factors with whatever support system is required to maintain the involvement and to guarantee continued development. In this country, there are heartening signs of movement toward the integration of normal and delayed children within early childhood education programs, such as Headstart. Emerging research on models of integrated education of preschool-age children, though sparse, is extremely encouraging (e.g., Bricker & Bricker, 1971, 1972). At this time, ENCOR staff are actively working with staffs of several local early education programs to implement the transfer of preschool-age delayed children into those normalized settings. We recognize, however, that a great deal of thought, planning, and interstaff preparation must precede systematic early educational integration. A resource-support system, designed to guarantee maintenance and growth of delayed children in normal education environments must be available and effective at the time of placement. The

model of the Developmental Center, as it is presently represented

in the ENCOR system, can be seen as a last-resort "platform"

supporting movement into more normalized educational services

(such as normal preschools, public school classes, vocational

training). We plan, however, that this model, because of segre-

gation factors, will become much more highly specialized and

less dominant with regard to the educational options we can offer

delayed children and their families in the near future.

The demand that a system plan for a continuity of service

types speaks to both inter-agency and intra-agency functions.

Inter-agency continuity refers to the linkup between different ser-

vice systems to assure client movement from one to the other.

Agency duplication of quality services, aside from being silly,

represents an unnecessary drain on both manpower and fiscal

resources. ENCOR places high value on coordinated efforts with

available generic services in the community (such as public

schools, YM/YWCA, normal preschools, private industry, welfare

programs, etc.). Intra-agency continuity related to the internal

design of continual service and support models that allow for effec-

tive training and efficient movement from one model to the next,

more advanced, component in the sequence. Continuity in the realm of residential services, for example, is especially critical for both children and adults. ENCOR has never incorporated the term "halfway home" into its vocabulary. The continuum between an institutional ward and a normal home or independent living can be broken down into many more chunks (and labeled appropriately) depending on client age and degree of training and support needs. Continuity of educational programs for children in ENCOR is evolving, including highly intense training programs (i. e., The Behavior Shaping Unit and The Developmental Maximation Unit), intermediate specialization (Developmental Centers), and supported alternatives (i. e., programs which are coordinated with normal early education programs, Headstart, public schools). Other unmet needs on the educational continuum are recognized and will have to evolve in the near future unless other community systems take the initiative. Figure 2 shows the current flow potential for continuity of developmental/educational services available through ENCOR.

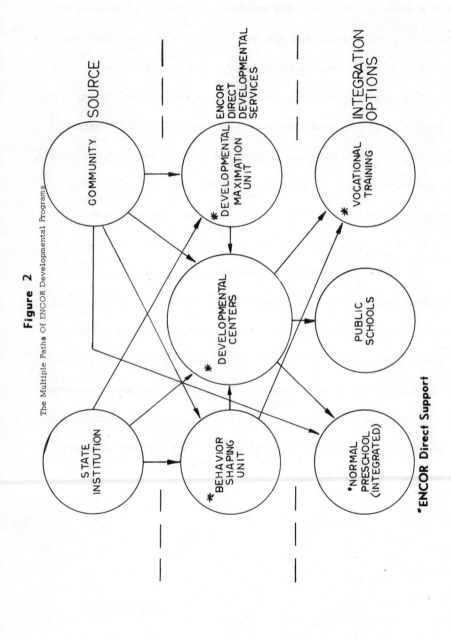

Figure 2

The Multiple Paths Of ENCOR Developmental Programs

COMMUNITY SOURCE

ENCOR DIRECT DEVELOPMENTAL SERVICES

INTEGRATION OPTIONS

DEVELOPMENTAL MAXIMATION UNIT

VOCATIONAL TRAINING

DEVELOPMENTAL CENTERS

PUBLIC SCHOOLS

STATE INSTITUTION

BEHAVIOR SHAPING UNIT

NORMAL PRESCHOOL (INTEGRATED)

*ENCOR Direct Support

Whether we're talking about inter- or intra- agency continuity, one objective must be constantly emphasized: mental retardation services systems should never allow a cul de sac program from which no advanced type exists or is planned. We should never plan the tragedy of a special education program which allows a delayed teenager to graduate into a life of boredom, dependency, and TV-watching.

In summary, although the principle of normalization, along with the corollaries it implies, is a recent innovation, it is not the exclusive property of mental retardation, as Wolfensberger (1972) clearly points out. Indeed, it should dictate service system designs and programs for all areas of handicap and "deviancy." In the area of MR services, the principle effectively assists us in the design of contexts of program operation. However, without innovation and skill at the program level, the normalization principle will wind up being a passing and empty promise which will only be of historical interest.

In the next section, I would like to share some ideas regarding fundamental educational values that I feel must be internalized by program administrators and client managers before technological skills can be truly productive.

FUNDAMENTAL EDUCATIONAL VALUES

All educators, but most especially those committed to facilitating the behavioral growth of developmentally delayed youngsters, must internalize and act upon a conscious set of basic values. Some of these values might be better described as "beliefs," others as "expectations" or "responsibilities." Whatever we call them, I am certain that program success (and, therefore, student growth) cannot be fully guaranteed without their implementation. The list that follows shouldn't be considered exhaustive; perhaps you can add a few of your own.

1. Intelligent optimism. After a talk I gave to a group of parents a while back, a mother approached me and asked me a question many of us have heard often, "Where can I have my son evaluated?" I asked her why she wanted the evaluation. "Well, " she replied, "I want to know what his potential is, what his limitations are." Such questions have come to trouble me deeply. I tried to explain to her that "evaluations" ought to be seen as assessment of the child's current level of development, and that it really wouldn't be fair to the youngster to assume any wide ranging limitations on his eventual development. Teachers, as well, are influ-

enced by this negative use of the term "potential." An example

of my concern is the five year old boy who entered our com-

munity services after having spent most of his first years

in the standard ward environment of our state institution.

As a child born with a rare form of hydrocephaly, barely

able to walk, unable to speak, he has been labeled as "severely

retarded" and was given a dismal prognosis for any eventual

development. After a year in one of our Developmental Centers

and living in a normalized home environment (an ENCOR

hostel), he was enrolled in a class for trainable children in

public school special education. Today he is succeeding in

school, walks very proficiently, and speaks in sentences.

He is now only "moderately retarded." What will his label

be a few years from now? Our experiences with Mike, partly

because his development was especially dramatic, have led

us to be even more cautious regarding statements of long-term

attainment and limitations. Was Mike "mis-evaluated"? I

think not. At the time of his initial evaluation, Mike met all

of the criteria necessary for the label that was assigned to him.

Rather I think that the assumptions regarding human develop-

ment on which such labeling processes are based are shaky

to say the least.

In the closing frames of an excellent film on training self-care skills (Genesis, 1971), the following words are superimposed over the face of a young retarded boy, "I was born a step behind, my only limitation is time. " I would prefer that our teachers assume that given enough time and skilled instruction, all of our students, including the profoundly retarded ones, could "catch up. " And, as our instructional skills improve, it should take less time to catch up. Teachers of retarded children must believe that the next small step in any child's development can be taken, even if we cannot always predict how long it will take to complete that step.

Accordingly, a teacher of delayed children must internalize two basic assumptions: (1) the child can learn, and (2) the teacher can be instrumental in that learning process. Without this prerequisite optimism, the following values reduce to empty rhetoric. Olshanky (1972) says it very nicely, "we still know very little about the process of changing behavior, and we still have very little firm knowledge which would justify an attitude of pessimism" (Page 157).

2. Educational Responsibility. Optimism alone will not get the job done. The teacher has to take responsibility for meeting instructional objectives or for adjusting those objectives when

they appear to have been defined inappropriately. When the children meet the educational goals set for them, the teacher has the right to receive credit for that accomplishment along with the child; but when the child does not meet the objective determined for him, it is the educational planners that must bear full responsibility and not the child. This philosophy guarantees some frustrations for teachers, but any other position opens the door for institutional alibis for failure. For too long, we in education have gotten away with taking credit for success -- and blaming the children for their failures. The whole list of psychological, neurological, and psycho-educational "diagnoses" has been used at one time or another to account for a child's failure to learn. (After all, he's retarded"; "What can I do, he is brain damaged" even, "You have to catch him when he is in a good mood.") Our shoulder-shrugs and our everyday conversation often reflect our failure to assume educational responsibility. Concepts such as "potential" and "limitations" should be more often directed to the state of our instructional skills than to the content of our students' heads and genes.

3. Common and Unique Objectives. All teachers of retarded

children must be familiar with the developmental "ladders" that children need to master in order to become more functionally independent and prepared for life in the community. The sequences of general skill mastery involved in motor, language, sensory-perceptual, and social development are moderately well understood at this point. Knowledge of these sequences helps us determine the next educational goal and to plan our overall curricula. Within the framework of the developmental scheme, we have to operate on the basis of each child's uniqueness and set his instructional objectives accordingly. These "individual" differences dictate both the effective ways in which the material is designed and presented, and demand effective motivational techniques which center on behavioral consequences and the way in which their functions are acquired. The education of retarded children requires an eye toward individually tailoring classroom consequences (Haughton, 1967) as well as attention toward programming curriculum on the basis of individual student performance.

Recently, one of our master teachers and her teaching staff at ENCOR's Benson Developmental Center developed a graphic way to focus the attention of both the teachers and the children's

parents on each child's common and unique educational goals.

As is the case in our other developmental centers, the ages of

the students at the Benson Center range from approximately 18

months to 15 years. Consequently, the long-term goals for each

student will vary according to his chronological age. Educational

objectives for those older youngsters, especially those who have

been eventual vocational training. Goals for others of the young-

sters involve placement in public schools. Finally, in the case

of the youngest children, the teachers hope to prepare the students

for acceptance into normal community pre-schools. In each case,

the next likely educational environment beyond the Developmental

Center has somewhat differing expectations and criteria for

admission. Examples of the objective displays appear in Figure 3.

Figure 3

Objective Displays of Developmental Objectives

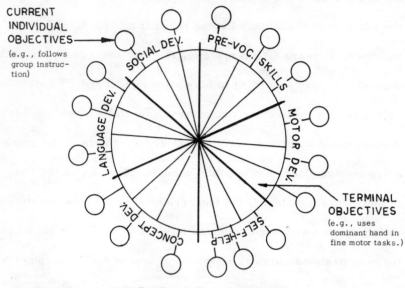

CURRENT
INDIVIDUAL
OBJECTIVES →
(e.g., follows
group instruc-
tion)

SOCIAL DEV.   PRE-VOC. SKILLS   MOTOR DEV.   SELF-HELP   CONCEPT DEV.   LANGUAGE DEV.

TERMINAL
OBJECTIVES
(e.g., uses
dominant hand in
fine motor tasks.)

WORKSHOP GOALS

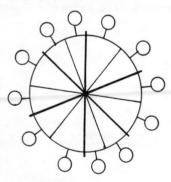

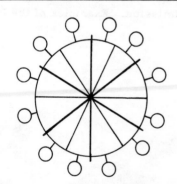

PRESCHOOL GOALS   PUBLIC SCHOOL GOALS

These simplified schematics show one way that common and unique developmental objectives can be displayed. The representative behaviors identified as "terminal objectives" can vary, depending on differences in expectancies in different communities. The wall-mounted displays can be further individualized by attaching a photograph of the child involved.

The next level of goal-setting involves the design of a developmental "pie", each major slice of which relates to one of the broad areas of human development (such as language development, motor development, etc.). Within each slice of the total pie, the teaching staff must agree upon behavioral objectives which represent achievement of some minimal criteria for that area of development. Finally, the developmental pies are individualized by extending from each slice a statement indicating the current and specific objective which the teacher is trying to reach with the child. By displaying developmental and individualized picture of educational goals, both the teachers and the children's parents can see at a glance where the child is currently performing and how far he has to go in order to meet the criteria for the long-term placement goals.

This idea for a graphic display of educational goals originated from a group of teachers and their supervisor, and by sharing their creative planning, this staff could see their ideas quickly disseminated among other similar facilities within the ENCOR system. Such innovativeness attests to the teachers' intense concern with common and unique educational objectives.

4. The Experimental Attitude in the Classroom. Visitors to our facilities often comment on the extent of decision-making responsibility assigned to the classroom teachers. True, we have no lock-step curriculum through which all our students and teachers must march. This state of affairs exists, in part, because no such "curriculum cook book" is available for severely and profoundly retarded children. In our attempts to improve our current state of educational planning, however, we should discern at least two levels of decision-making. At one level, we must decide on a sequence of <u>program objectives</u> (e. g. , "discriminates the words <u>big</u> and <u>little</u>" or"speaks in in two word sentences, noun plus verb"). The design of over-all sequences of program objectives ("ladders") may be quite involved and be the result of a level of child development scholarships that cannot be expected of every classroom teacher. It is neither fair or reasonable to expect each teacher to design elaborate sequences of such objectives to

cover all the broad areas of child development. In addition, broad developmental program objectives should be standard for all our retarded students, with each student fitting into a sequence at some point on the continuum.

The second level of decision-making relates to <u>instructional procedures</u>, involving both the determination of immediate, individualized objectives and the selection of the educational methods most likely to be successful in achieving the immediate objective. It is at this second decision level that maximum flexibility and latitude must be reserved for the teacher. It is here that the teacher must "experiment" with each child to discover the most effective materials, instructions, and behavioral consequences that will hasten the learning process and eventual movement through the sequence of program objectives.

An experimental approach means, simply, the systematic exploration of new ideas, and does not exclude any hypothesis-generating philosophy of education. In fact, we have teachers in our program who come from a wide variety of background and who have a wide variety of teaching philosophies. A Montessori-trained teacher can be as probing and experimental as one whose training has been in the area of behavior analysis. By precluding individuals who represent certain philosophical orientations, we may be losing exciting new innovations in the effective education of delayed children. A dynamic educational program should be flexible enough to incorporate such teacher variability, but also require that each teacher demonstrate accountability through growth in student performance. In no case should "experimentalism" become a euphemism for chaos or a cover for dogmatism.

5. Charting the Course of Human Growth. In order to realize the values discussed above, teachers and others concerned with student growth need a set of tools which allow them to magnify and project that growth. If we cannot see and remember behavioral change - even when it's occurring - it's difficult to maintain a spirit of optimism. If we are ignorant of individual performance levels and trends, we cannot completely fulfill our responsibility for each student. Once educational objectives are identified, only the child can tell us whether our selections were wise, and only then through his behavior over time. Finally, if we expect teachers to probe and experiment for better ways to help their students develop, we must insure that they have tools available which assist them to be careful and systematic in their daily explorations. ENCOR staff in

all program areas, especially in our educational services, are using the system of precision teaching to chart and project client growth toward more normalizing behavioral objectives. Since this system is a central ingredient of the educational services provided by ENCOR, I will briefly review its origin and applicability.

In 1965, O. R. Lindsley and his students at the University of Kansas began developing a system of data-based instruction that came to be called "Precision Teaching". Precision Teaching began to evolve after it was recognized that classroom teachers need to maintain direct and continuous measurement of their students' behavioral growth if individually-tailored education were to become anything more than vacuous slogan. At least three basic prerequisites seem to be important considerations: first, performance measurement techniques have to be offered to teachers in such a way that teachers can independently maintain the individualized measurements without having to rely on "trained observers" who are natural inhabitants of the classroom ecology. Secondly, the format of the measurement system should be standardized in order to maximize communications among teachers, parents, and resource personnel. Finally, the measurement of classroom performance should help to involve more dynamically

the teacher and her children in flexible educational planning.
Integrated measurement must facilitate the learning process and
not serve solely as an historical record of success or failure.
As a result, the performance measurement system must involve
frequent monitoring of individual progress. The four basic steps
in implementing Precision Teaching are the following: (A) Pinpoint.
In any problem-solving endeavor, the first step involves defining
the subject-matter. In precision teaching, pinpointing refers to
the specification of the behavioral movement cycle which the
student is currently exhibiting too often or not often enough. The
objective is defined, then, in terms of accelerating or decelerating
the pinpoint. For example, an academic pinpoint might be "Tommy
points to the named picture card" or "Mary correctly imitates a
vowel sound." Management pinpoints are usually those movements
which interfere with desirable development or are dangerous to the
student or others. Examples of these deceleration pinpoints might
be "Jane strikes other children" and "Kenny falls on floors and
cries." The emphasis, however, is always on the acquisition and
strengthening of those behaviors involved in normal development.
It is stressed to the staff that the tools of precision teaching are
not to be used as we would a fire extinguisher, only in times of

crisis. (B) Record and Chart. The second calls for the manager to count each occurrence of the pinpoint and to record the amount of time (in minutes) that the observation period consumed. For some academic pinpoints, the observation period might be as brief as one minute. Certain management pinpoints might require a watchful eye for the entire school day. The time dimension of the recording is critical, because it allows us to derive a sensitive datum of performance: frequency (movement cycles per minute). The student's performance frequency is then transferred to a standardized behavior chart to provide both the teacher and her student with a visual summary of the student's growth over time (usually calendar days). The display helps the teacher chart an educational course for the student, to determine conditions and procedures which facilitate adequate growth, and to compare the progress of different students in the same curriculum areas. (C) Change. When the chart indicates that the student is not being responsive to the educational environment arranged for him, it is the teachers responsibility to decide what changes in that environment might better support the individual student's growth (procedural decision-making). Since precision teaching is a system of measurement and not a theory of remediation, any theory can contribute hypotheses for the best change plan. The only requirement is that the change plan lend itself to replication, and that it be described in a way understandable to all. The teacher might appeal to Montessori, Piaget, B. F. Skinner or Zen Buddhism for the source of her ideas which is fine, as long as she can describe what she is doing in basic English. By being descriptive with regards to educational objectives and procedures, we can all share our personal expertise and success.

(D) Try, try again. Finally, we must confront the painful reality that our first guesses are not always successful. Often, though, teachers are not aware of the number of options for change plans that they control (or could control). A change might be as simple as scheduling a certain activity at a different time of day, or in a different place. Change might involve providing the student with feedback of a different form of frequency. The curriculum material and form of verbal instruction might be modified: ad infinitum. Thus, the final step in precision teaching says, "keep trying." When trying to teach retarded children, this final request is particularly important because the teacher has to rely so much on her own wits. (For other references on precision teaching, see Jordan & Robbins, 1972; Loeing, 1972; Lindsley, 1971, 1972; Pennypacker, Koenig, & Lindsley, 1972).

An example which illustrates the five fundamental educational values just reviewed -- with a major focus on precision teaching is presented below.

ENCOR example: Ginny's blouse. One of our very fine teachers is Ginny Carter, a young woman whose cheerfulness and commitment to her students is a joy to behold. As with all of our teaching staff, she has assumed responsibility for charting critical pinpoints for each of her children. The project represented below is one Ginny shared with me not too long ago.

One of Ginny's students, Richard, is a very delayed youngster who displays minimal receptive language skills. A major goal Ginny set for Richard was to teach him to identify objects in his environment by pointing to them when they were named. Because of the severity of Richard's delay, Ginny discovered that her first objective was to have Richard place his hand on a notebook (modeling). Ginny recorded a daily one-minute sample of Richard's responses to this request without assistance and each time he placed his hand anywhere other than on the notebook. The frequencies of Richard's correct and incorrect hand placement are shown in Figures 4(A) and 4 (B). The dots are correct responses, and the "x's" are incorrect responses.

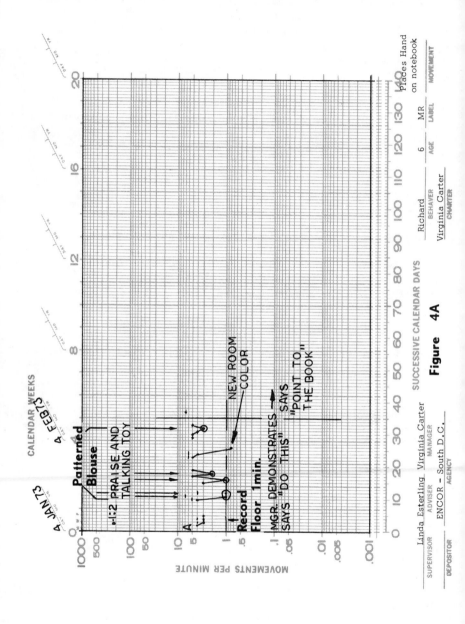

Figure 4A

108

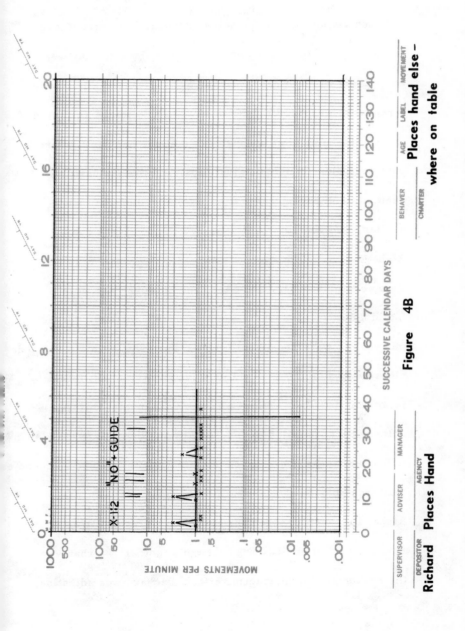

Figure 4B

For the first five timings, Richard was doing quite well. But then his correct frequencies dropped considerably (e. g., the first two circled frequencies). Over the following weekend, Ginny worried over what might have caused this interference with Richard's progress. The only things she could think of as being a bit unusual was that she had worn colorful, patterned blouses on those two days, and that Richard had seemed to be paying more attention to her blouses than to her face and voice. Could it be...? Through the chart, Richard gave us the answer. As you, too, can see, when Ginny systematically varied the type of blouse she wore (solid color vs. patterns), Richard's frequencies of correct movements were consistently lower when she wore a patterned blouse. And on the day Ginny moved him into a different room that had walls with concrete blocks painted different colors, Richard failed to respond at all. But wait, what else is Richard telling us? If you connect only the circled frequencies (patterned blouse days), what do you see? Try it. Yes, Richard's correct movements were accelerating! What a relief for all of us (including Richard's mother) -- whatever the reason for the distracting effect, Richard was adjusting to it over time. One of the joys of precision teaching is the potential it allows us for discovering dimension of children's behavior through what the children are telling us. Of course, the tools of precision teaching work best in the hand of creative probing teachers like Ginny who refused to dismiss Richard's down days as attributable to "bad mood" or "something that must have happened at home." And when we say that a child is "tuning out," it's more likely that we're simply ignorant of what he is "tuning in" to.

Summary. At this point, it appears that the potential applications of precision teaching are virtually unlimited. Slowly, our group is beginning to explore variations in the theme--identifying and charting such pinpoints as inter-staff behavior (e.g., asks assistance, gives assistance, shares chart), personal inner behavior (e.g., work-related "uppers" and "downers"), already available budget and payroll information (e.g., facility per diems, absenteeism, and others). We'll probably chart some blind alleys, but I think we'll hit pay dirt often enough to help us better understand and plan for our students' behavioral growth, our interpersonal behaviors, and our personal thoughts and feelings. Precision teaching is perhaps one way to join the skills of behaviorism with the values of humanism. And perhaps the distinction was never real, anyway.

THE BEST FOR LAST: PARENT PARTNERSHIPS

In the case that anyone questions it, it is important to emphasize that positive consumer involvement is the life ring around community programs for retarded persons. The functions that organized parents can fulfill vis-a-vis service agencies include at least the following five.

1) Interpretation of the agency to the community at large. The strategies and tactics of a community service agency may be disputed or confusing for a large segment of the non-retarded citizenry, especially those not personally acquainted with retarded people. And the credibility of most "professionals" is often pre-tainted, almost by cultural definition. The jargon of professionals loses something in the translation to common English, as well. But parents can usually be suspected of only one type of self-interest: the need for quality services for their offspring. It seems natural, then, that the voice of an affected parent should ring more true than that of a paid professional.

2) Protection of agency continuity. At a time of high competition for limited fiscal resources, political and moral support by service consumers aids immeasurably in assuring the

continuity and expansion of programs. Politicians at all levels of government - federal, state, and local - have said that a letter from an involved parent has a much greater impact than a similar plea from a paid professional. And if messages of support and demand come from active consumer organizations the impact is heightened. However, parents are not dumb, and in order to generate and sustain enthusiastic, vocal support, agency workers must produce and be in a position to demonstrate their value to service consumers. Close communication and honest sharing provide the foundation for that demonstration.

3) Quality-control monitors of existing services. In addition to having representation on policy-making bodies and advisory boards, parent organizations (such as local Associations for Retarded Children) can develop "task forces" whose responsibility it is to inspect and review specific program types. For example, our Greater Omaha Association for Retarded Children has created several task forces for the various service components of ENCOR. If organized well, these groups have a reward as well as a critical function. As one whose programs have been "monitored," I can report that it isn't always fun - I've had to answer to some probing criticism. But in each of

the few instances, I have valued the questions (even when they were a bit embarrassing). It's all too easy to overlook program stagnation. If anything keeps us from evolving into the "typical bureaucracy," it will be the monitoring function provided by independent consumer organizations.

4) Stimulus for agency self-renewal. ENCOR staff are continually reminded that were it not for parents - through their Greater Omaha ARC - the agency would not exist. In 1968, GOARC stated some model programs which were turned over to the new agency, ENCOR, in mid-1970. At that time, GOARC returned to being a poorer, but still dynamic organization running volunteer programs (Pilot Parents, Citizens Advocacy, Youth ARC, etc.) to parallel the funded operations of ENCOR. The consumers, then, fathered the service agency and quickly kicked it out of the nest. Since 1970, GOARC and ENCOR have maintained a relationship which has certainly enriched both groups. Gentle pressure from GOARC people has caused new ENCOR program models to evolve faster than they might have. If we hope to meet the special needs of all retarded people in the community, it helps to be encouraged and reminded to plan for the needs yet unmet. For example, at the first GOARC meeting my wife and I attended, a certain

mother asked when the Behavior Shaping Unit might be expected to open. Her son was then in the state institution, and she clearly pointed out the reason that he would need the sort of training environment in our then proposed Behavior Shaping Unit -- and she wanted him back in his hometown. At each meeting thereafter, I came to expect the same gentle, but firm, inquiry. I am convinced that I worked harder to get that unit started because of this persistent lady! When the unit finally opened, her son was in the first group to enter from the institution. Responsiveness to unmet consumer needs and constantly searching for better models builds a stronger, ever-renewing agency.

5) Educational partners. Most of the time, professionals think of educating parents as a unilateral process in which the pro gives the parent information, as in a traditional teacher-student relationship. Not nearly often enough do we conceive of structuring reciprocal knowledge-sharing processes, say, in which a child's teacher shares ways of teaching him with parents, and, in turn, the parents share their relevant knowledge with the child's teachers. In such a situation, the role of student and teacher shifts back and forth dynamically. Over the last couple of years, Kay

Galloway and I have looked into the possibility of offering
parents classes in the home application of precision teaching
(Galloway & Galloway, 1971; Galloway, 1972). The classes
we have helped organized through ENCOR have continued to
provide rewarding experiences for us, the ENCOR teachers,
and the participating parents. The purpose of precision
teaching classes for parents is to share tools related to
careful observation, continuous counting and charting of
important behavior and creating systematic change plans -
tools that the teachers are already applying during the child's
day programs. In these settings, parents are encouraged to
choose behavioral targets, set up their projects, and select
effective change plans that might better assist the child to
reach educational goals. Initially, the child's teacher
advises and guides the parents while they are learning the
basic mechanics of precision teaching.

Let me share an actual parent project with you as a case in
point. The parents of one of our clients, Shirley, attended
classes offered parents from ENCOR's South Developmental
Center. Shirley had many areas of her behavior that needed
to be altered and/or strengthened. Her parents decided to
concentrate on fine-motor, pre-writing skills, selecting

tracing letters as their pinpoint. More specifically, they defined a correct movement cycle as tracing a "stroke" of the letter without deviating from the faint line provided (e. g. , the letter "H" could have three correct strokes). The first practice sheet had letters to be traced, all of which involved straight lines (I, T, X, L, V, H, F). The parents worked with Shirley 10 minutes a day and counted the number of correct and incorrect strokes traced during that timing. The chart of Shirley's progress, created by her parents is shown in Figures 5 (A) and 5 (B).

While Shirley was trying hard to do well, her parents praised her each time she traced a letter correctly; later on, they praised her when she completed about 15 letters well. Poorly traced letters were simply crossed out immediately. After Shirley had reached a fair degree of competency, her parents moved on to a new set of letters to be traced (N, A, Z, E, K, M, O). As the chart indicates, Shirley's errors increased for a time, but she quickly became accurate on the new set of letters.

In some people's eyes, this project may seem trivial - but not so for this youngster's parents. Perhaps for the first time, they knew that they could be as influential on

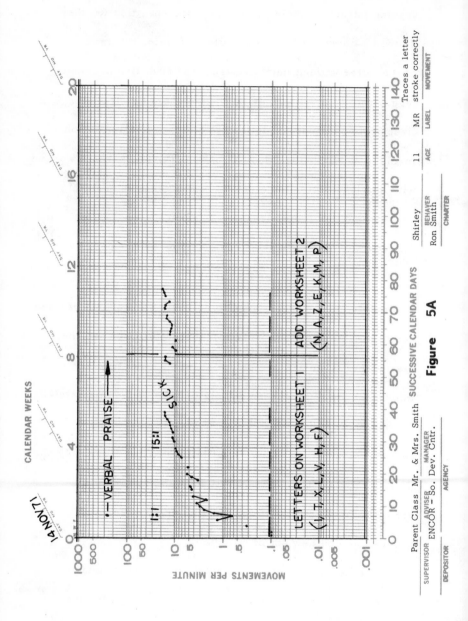

Figure 5A

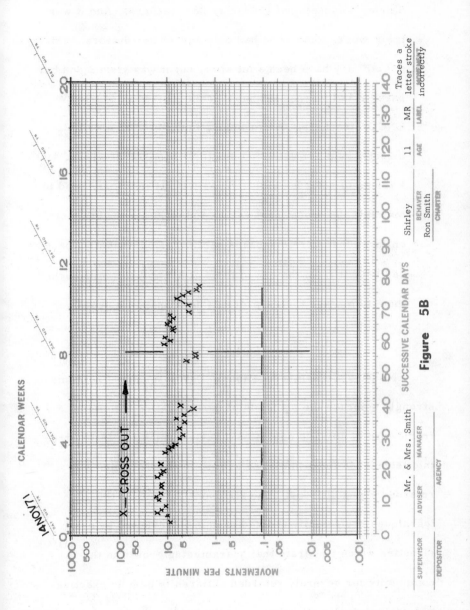

Figure 5B

Shirley's educational growth as her teachers. And it was their work; some of us had only served as advisors. Shirley's growth may have been a bit slow, but it was visible and her parents had learned the basic tools utilized by Shirley's ENCOR teachers. Accordingly, they too were able to directly help her grow and see their own effectiveness.

Parents of retarded children, as well as teachers, need to maintain the educational values and attitudes toward their children that were discussed earlier. Consequently, parents can benefit from the use of tools at home that better enable them to manage their children's developmental growth.

CONCLUSION

ENCOR's modern, educational, Developmental Programs strongly embrace the principle of normalization within the framework of specific educational values which are translated into techniques for stimulating growth in severely mentally retarded young citizens. The atmosphere in which these techniques are actually utilized have been reviewed by case vignettes which illustrate that guaranteeing growth in the community for severely retarded children is both an exacting and professionally stimulating challenge!

120

REFERENCES

Bricker, D. & Bricker, W. Toddler research and intervention project, report-year 1. IMRID Behavioral Monograph (No. 20). Nashville, Tennessee: George Peabody College for Teachers, 1971.

Bricker, D. & Bricker, W. Toddler research and intervention project report-year II. IMRID Behavioral Monograph (No. 21). Nashville, Tennessee: George Peabody College for Teachers, 1972.

Dybwad, G. Action implications, U.S.A. today. In R. B. Kugel & W. Wolfensberger (Eds.), Changing patterns in residential services for the mentally retarded. Washington: President's Committee on Mental Retardation, 1969.

Galloway, C. Precision parents and the development of retarded behavior. In J. B. Jordan & L. S. Robbins (Eds.), Let's try doing something else kind of thing: Behavioral principles and the exceptional child. Arlington, Virginia: The Council for Exceptional Children, 1972.

Galloway, C. & Galloway, K. Parent classes in precise behavior management. Teaching Exceptional Children, 1971, 3, 120-128.

GENESIS. Baltimore: Hallmark Films, Inc., 1971.

Haughton, E. A practical way of individually tailoring classroom consequences. Unpublished doctoral dissertation, University of Kansas, 1967.

Jordan, J. B. & Robbins, L. S. (Eds.), Let's try doing something else kind of thing: Behavioral principles and the exceptional child. Arlington, Virginia: The Council for Exceptional Children, 1972.

Koenig, C. H. Charting the future course of behavior. Kansas City, Kansas: Precision Media, 1972.

Kugel, R. B. & Wolfensberger, W. (Eds.), Changing patterns in residential services for the mentally retarded. Washington: President's Committee on Mental Retardation, 1969.

Kuhn, T. S. The structure of scientific revolutions. Chicago: The University of Chicago Press, 1962.

Lindsley, O. R. Precision teaching in perspective. An interview with Ogden R. Lindsley. Teaching Exceptional Children, 1971, 3, 114-119.

Lindsley, O. R. From Skinner to precision teaching: The child knows best. In J. B. Jordan & L. S. Robbins (Eds.), Let's try doing something else kind of thing: Behavioral principles and the exceptional child. Arlington, Virginia: The Council for Exceptional Children, 1972.

National Association for Retarded Children , Policy Statement on Residential Care, 1972.

Olshansky, S. Changing vocational behavior through normalization. In W. Wolfensberger, The principle of normalization in human services. Toronto: National Institute on Mental Retardation, 1972.

Pennsylvania Association for Retarded Children vs. the Commonwealth of Pennsylvania, 1971.

Pennypacker, H. S., Koenig, C. H., & Lindsley, O. R. Handbook of the standard behavior chart, (Preliminary edition). Kansas City, Kansas: Precision Media, 1972.

Wolfensberger, W. The origin and nature of our institutional models. In R. B. Kugel & W. Wolfensberger (Eds.), Changing patterns in residential services for the mentally retarded. Washington: President's Committee on Mental Retardation, 1969.

Wolfensberger, W. The principle of normalization in human services. Toronto: National Institute on Mental Retardation, 1972.

Wyatt vs. Stickney, Civil Suit #3195-N, State of Alabama, 1972.

ENCOR: SOME PROGRAMS AND THEIR CLIENTS
Robert Coleman

The Developmental Maximation Unit is a cornerstone of ENCOR's system of community services, for its success in developing the potential of persons with the most limited repertoire of abilities has been a validation of ENCOR's developmental model. In its one and one-half years of existence, the DMU has graduated 18 persons to more normal modes of community living.

The residents of the DMU are severely and profoundly retarded persons with complex medical and developmental disorders. Ordinarily, such persons would be guaranteed custodial care and the institutional maintenance of their lives. By contrast, in the bright and homelike atmosphere of the DMU, they receive from the specialized staff a wide variety of developmental therapies to stimulate the growth of their auditory, visual and motor skills. Unless medical considerations forbid it, residents of the DMU attend ENCOR developmental centers or the appropriate facilities in the community.

The unique achievement of ENCOR's Developmental Maximation Unit has been to combine medical care for complex developmental disorders with a system of community services for retarded persons. The bridge between the DMU and the community has been the developmental model, by which the perhaps unseen potential of severely retarded persons can be nourished to its fullest growth by love and by knowledge.

127

Frequently, handicapped children are excluded from public school
education because of their lack of self-help skills and a delay in
motor and language development. ENCOR's Developmental Centers
accept all handicapped children up to twelve years of age, and work
to bring each child to the fullest development of his potential. The
child's developmental goals are first assessed and then revised as
the child progresses; teaching begins at the child's level of self-help,
motor, concept, language and social development. These skills
are enlarged and refined until the child, hopefully, reaches that
level of development where he can attend a regular pre-school or
public school special education program.

The ENCOR Family Services Division has placed many severely handicapped children in developmental homes since the concept was put into practice two years ago. Essentially, the developmental home is a marriage of the concepts of adoption and foster care, for developmental parents are expected to make a commitment to raise their foster child to adulthood. Developmental parents are trained to understand retardation and the concept of normalization, as well as to deal with the emotional and physical problems of their child. After placement, the family is strongly supported by the Family Services Division.

The Coordinated Early Education Program (CEEP) is ENCOR's most innovative approach to "normalizing" the early education of retarded children. This program places developmentally delayed children among their age-peers in normal community educational settings. CEEP, one year old in March, 1974, now operates in six Omaha pre-school day-care centers, and serves forty children. Further expansion is planned through partial support of a grant from the Federal Bureau of Education for the Handicapped.

Children of all ages, as education specialists have long recognized but only lately put into practice, learn a great deal from interaction with their peers. There is the added recognition that the early educational experiences of the retarded child can enable him to loosen the bonds of his developmental handicap. As the CEEP program is proving, the delayed child can, through imitation, striving, and an enriched program, develop his physical and mental abilities to unexpected levels, simply out of his need for social contact with his age-mates.

Two ENCOR teachers are assigned to the five to eight delayed children in each early education center. They use precision teaching to observe, chart, and monitor the progress of each child; teachers also provide individualized learning programs and speech therapy. Their task is primarily to direct and refine the child's skills; the motivation behind the growing skills springs less from their teaching than from the normal milieu of children learning from each other.

ENCOR does not pick a "poster child", but if one were to be chosen, it would probably be Jenny. More than any other client, Jenny's condition has demanded the full range of ENCOR's services; few other clients have refuted a gloomy prognosis with more inspiring progress.

Jenny was born with hydrocephalus and spinal irregularities, to the extent that profound retardation was forecast. A series of complex operations and physical discomfort kept Jenny in a kind of developmental limbo for almost two years. But since coming to the DMU in November, 1972, Jenny's development and learning have been astonishing. At the age of three, she now feeds herself, has a vocabulary of more than sixty recognizable words, and, despite her partial paralysis below the waist, can go where she pleases by crawling. Recently, she received her own wheelchair and has learned to operate it.

During the day, Jenny attends the Early Learning Place, an Omaha pre-school that takes part in the CEEP program. This experience, and the speech therapy given by her ENCOR teacher, has vastly expanded her social and language skills. With the greater mobility of her wheelchair, and the stimulus of a normal school environment, Jenny's development, like that of any three-year-old, is just beginning.

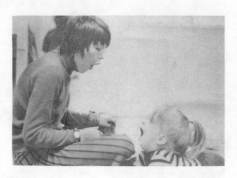

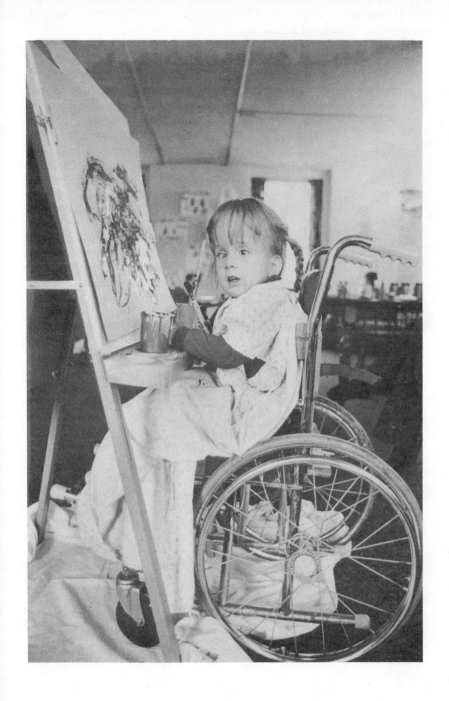

Elaine is ten years old, attends a developmental center, and lives at ENCOR's Behavior Shaping Unit. Although she still has moments of frightened withdrawal, Elaine is very attached to, and curious about, her teachers at the BSU. In one year of living at the unit, Elaine has learned to accept other people, and has lost many of her self-stimulating and destructive behaviors.

Supervised by Behavioral Specialists, teachers at the BSU use the charting and observation techniques of precision teaching and the reinforcement methods of behavior modification to eliminate the bizarre, self-destructive, and inappropriate behaviors of ENCOR clients. The behaviors, such as head-banging and autism, are often strongly entrenched, but the progress made in their elimination by use of these techniques is concrete and encouraging.

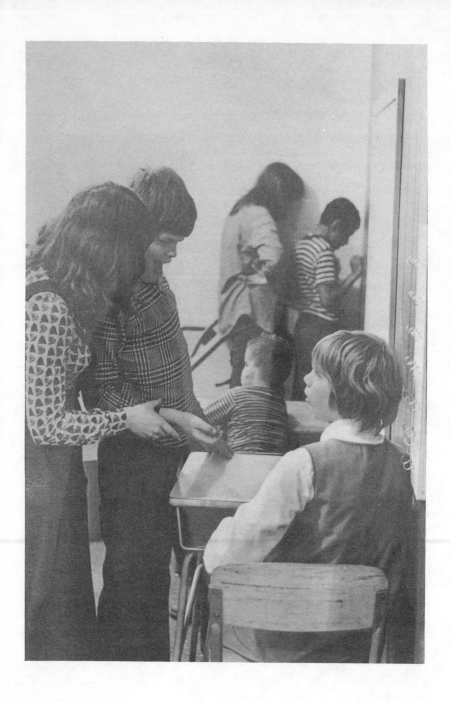

The purpose of ENCOR's Adolescent Education program is to graduate handicapped students twelve years of age and older to more normal educational and vocational programs. Teachers continue to work on fundamentals of writing and counting, but place an appropriate stress on social behavior and pre-vocational learning.

The five Vocational Services Centers in ENCOR's system receive
clients sixteen years and older, many of whom are newly released
from institutions. At the centers, they receive an evaluation and
refinement of their work skills, training in academic and social
skills, if necessary, as well as the opportunity of full-time paid
work. Clients work on a variety of contracts solicited from industry,
which entail the sorting and assembly of manufactured and industrial
parts and items. For some clients, the vocational centers are a long
term place of employment; for others, it is the first stop on the road
to normal employment.

Another step towards vocational autonomy are the ENCOR work stations, which provide paid on-the-job training in several manufacturing and service industries. Clients work under normal industrial supervision with support services available to them. At the end of the three-month training period, most clients seek and gain jobs in the mainstream of society.

CHALLENGES IN PROGRAM IMPLEMENTATION WITHIN INSTITUTIONS FOR THE RETARDED

Kenneth D. Keith and *Hugh M. Sage*

In this presentation, my colleague and I will initially survey some of the recurring problems pf institutional program implementation within the areas of values, goals, expectations, and administrative contingencies. We will focus on two methods which have been involved in the derivation of goals: a priori judgements and empirical analysis. We will also examine the propriety of expectations of institutional personnel with respect to residents and staff. Lastly, we shall discuss the essential components of an alternative management system which involves the application of empirically derived behavioral techniques to the development and maintenance of staff behavior.

Even a cursory review of recent literature reveals a good deal of dissatisfaction with institutions for the retarded. Much of the controversy seems to center on the values and goals, the expectations, and the administrative styles of institutions as reflected by the activities of their personnel. Impetus for change has been great, largely due to grass-root and legislative support for humanistic and habilitative programs, and to the evolution of an effective behavioral technology. These problem areas are a major source of concern for those who must implement institutional programs, as well as for extra-institutional observers. We will present here an exploration of these problems, from the viewpoint of institutional implementation.

Value and Goals

Where do institutional goals come from? At least two alternative possibilities present themselves. First, goals may be a logical function of empirical analyses of intra- and extra-institutional contexts, in relation to the behavior, health, and general well-being of retarded persons. That is, goals are derived from a critical study of needs, deficits, values, resources, ideologies, etc. Second, goals may arise from assumptions and values which are held a priori, and which are not considered amenable to examination. Unfortunately, the latter seems all too often to be the case. It should be noted that several other alternate sources of goals are specific cases of the two noted. It is not uncommon for professional staff to attribute goals to other people, especially to administrators. For example, when asked on a questionnaire to describe how objectives were derived for their unit, professionals tended to accept objectives uncritically as "givens", without reference to how they were derived, how they were to be achieved, or how they would benefit residents. In such a case, the goal statement may be traced to its original source, which in all likelihood will approximate one of the two processes noted. This does not preclude the possibility that goals may sometimes be derived from some combination of these processes.

Is there really a viable alternative to the uncritical, a priori acceptance of values and, hence, goals? We believe that there is. First our assumptions and values, whatever their basis, are frequently translated directly into goal statements. Thus, if we are "believers" in a particular treatment, technique or philosophy, we may move immediately and mistakenly to the goal of widespread implementation. However, we believe that it is considerably more useful to begin by stating the implications of assumptions in the form of testable propositions. In this way, the validity of values may be examined empirically and be reference to the consequences of specific instances of implementation.

Skinner has clarified this issue somewhat by conceptualizing value statements as rough descriptions of contingencies. A value statement or assumption implies that a) certain activities are (ought to be) carried out, and b) the consequences of doing so are desirable (reinforcing). Values may be seen, therefore, as descriptions of means-consequences relationships and as such must be revised if the description is not accurate. A recent study by Schaefer and Martin provided a dramatic example which illustrates this point. They described a hospital setting in which a group of nurses seemed to believe in the provision of indiscriminate love to children (a value). It shortly became apparent that the nurses, in providing indiscriminate love (comfort, candy, etc), were systematically teaching some children to be severe headbangers. However, when the means-consequences description was revised (i.e., "Discriminate displays of affection strengthen the behaviors which produce them"), the basis for more effective treatment was provided. Good intentions are just not enough!

Interpersonal Expectations

It has been clearly demonstrated that the expectancies which a person has, and the expectations which others have for him, may be important determinants of behavior. However, untested assumptions and inappropriate expectations are sometimes applied to both residents and staff in institutional settings. A number of factors have sometimes led institutional staff members to seriously under-estimate the learning potential of retardates, particularly those behaving within the severe and profound ranges. An important problem was the lack, until recent years, of effective behavioral technologies for dealing with the special problems of retarded persons (i.e., the learning literature in retardation was virtually negligible prior to the late 1950's). Consequently, it is not surprising that, although inservice training programs have existed for over a century, they have been (and frequently remain) deficient in the provision of adequate skills to enable staff members to effectively habilitate their residents. Given the aforementioned conditions, administrative contingencies within institutions have frequently made it most adaptive for staff members to assume those roles for which they were most competent (i.e., custodial, protective, medical-oriented tasks).

A second major impact of illicit expectations (and one which is frequently overlooked) is that resulting from the low esteem accorded direct-care personnel by many professionals and administrators. For example, Shafter (1971) has noted that the dehumanization of institutional residents cannot be overcome until the dehumanization of staff is stopped. Roos (1970) has pointed out that, "Professionals tend to perceive the workers as ignorant, custodial, and in constant need of training and supervision"(p. 46). Despite increasing lip service to "democratic" administrative arrangements, direct-care personnel (much less residents) are rarely involved in important decision-making, and heavy emphasis is placed upon rules, regulations, and job descriptions in controlling aide behavior.

We do not believe aides to be ignorant, unreliable, or unskillful. A multitude of recent reports of behavior modification projects suggests that direct-care personnel can learn to effect significant resident progress. It is logical to assume, in fact, that such progress *must* be achieved by aides. In recognition of this fact, but with the prior reservations about the aides' limitations still in mind, many institutions have typically attempted a compromise: Allow the professional to solve the problems, and assign to the aide the task of implementing the solution. The futility of such an approach has been recognized, and Gardner (1971) has offered an optimistic alternative: that direct-care staff *can* become effective, independent problem-solvers. The implementation of this optimistic alternative requires an analysis of administrative contingencies.

Administrative Contingencies

Generally speaking, behaviors which are reinforced are more likely to recur, while those which are ignored or punished are to varying degrees less likely to recur. This principle is seldom used effectively in institutional management where, as

Gardner (1971) has noted, relevant feedback is infrequently provided in the area of resident progress. Thus, staff members may be reinforced (or punished) for behaviors in such areas as personal appearance, personality, and seniority, while specific resident-oriented habilitative behaviors are virtually ignored. This leads, in all likelihood, to the literal extinction of the skills, creativity, and initiative which are so crucial to the success of direct-care personnel. It is sometimes suggested that staff members should perform assigned tasks simply because they are part of a job description or because they are consistent with the goals and objectives of the agency. Those who hold such a view would be wise to note that leading proponents of objective-based management systems do not concur.

Nor can training alone solve the problems of implementation. One hears much about the training of staff, and relatively little about the steps which must be taken to insure that staff will maintain and utilize their skills. People engage in behavior, and it produces consequences, while working, playing, caring for themselves or others; whether applying themselves diligently, or loafing on the job. It has been noted that the consequences influence the subsequent behavior of the individual, and that the work setting must be viewed as a learning environment*. Yet we continue to manage working environment in direct contradiction to these principles. We have been, in essence, willing to apply what we have learned about human behavior to retardates, but not to ourselves.

An additional rationale for the failure to reinforce and attend to staff behavior is reflected in the contention that the satisfaction of caring for residents and seeing them progress should maintain appropriate performance. Available evidence seems to refute this argument, possibly due to the long periods of time which are sometimes required to effect significant change with the severely and profoundly retarded. Thus, additional sources of reinforcement are necessary, such as the facilitative effects of relevant professional feedback upon the behavior of institutional staff. However, when feedback is given in institutional settings, it is frequently punitive in quality, and is often contingent upon behavior in areas of minimal or questionable relevance to resident habilitation. It has been observed, for example, that institutional merit systems have had a tendency to regard tenure, as opposed to achievement.

*For example, Odiorne (1965) stated in <u>Management by Objectives</u> that "The changing of individual behavior is a function of the individual's receiving a series of reinforcers for small stages of development of the new behavior" (p. 116).

A Proposed Solution

An alternative management system, involving the provision
or relevant feedback, is within the bounds of currently available
behavioral technology. Its essential components will be summarized here.

First, a re-ordering of the interaction of institutional
professionals and administrators with direct-care personnel
will be required. If supervisors reinforce custodial or other
non-habilitative activities more effectively than training efforts,
we could predict a higher frequency of non-habilitative staff
behaviors. On the other hand, if supervisors interact with aids
in a manner which identifies and reinforces requisite habilitative
behaviors, those efforts are likely to be strengthened. Professional and administrative personnel must also selectively attend
to and reinforce staff behaviors which approximate the desired
skills, as a means of shaping them. When the skills have been
developed, they must be maintained in the same way. Abundant
evidence of the efficacy of such an approach with the mentally ill
has been provided in our state by Dr. Jay M. Toews and his
associates at the Lincoln Regional Center.

Second, direct-care personnel may possess the requisite
skills, but lack the time and other resources to perform certain

aspects of ongoing analysis and decision-making. In such instances, technical assistance in data collection and processing, and in the provision of relevant information from the data, may be required.

Third, the procedure used to evaluate the performance of personnel must be specifically and objectively concerned with discriminating and measuring relevant resident-oriented services. Accordingly, evaluation should be a continuous process, providing data which can serve as a guide for the shaping of staff behavior; annual point-in-time evaluation cannot provide data upon which reliable ongoing program decisions can be made.

Finally, the various extrinsic benefits (e.g., promotion, salary increases, status) which are available within the organization must be made contingent upon relevant resident-oriented behaviors, as opposed to tenure, personal appearance, attendance, etc. That is, "success on the job" should truly be determined by the aide's ability to provide good training, personal care, and his general effectiveness in arranging an environment which is reinforcing and useful for the resident.

Conclusion

Institutions have long offered "services" for the retarded, but have failed to habilitate the majority of their residents--especially the severely and profoundly retarded. Today, there is much pressure for the humanization of residential facilities, and an effective behavioral technology is at hand. Much emphasis has been placed upon the application of this technology to the behavior of residents, with little given to the changes which are required in staff behavior. That is, there is little evidence to suggest that the technology has been effectively used to shape and maintain requisite staff skills. Yet, this is an alternative which seems likely to be useful to institutional personnel as they become increasingly accountable for habilitative functions on behalf of the severe and profoundly retarded.

REFERENCES

Bensberg, G. J. & Barnett, C. D. Attendant training in southern residential facilities for the mentally retarded. Atlanta, Ga.: Southern Regional Education Board, 1966.

Blatt, B. Purgatory. In R. Kugel & W. Wolfensberger (Eds.), Changing patterns in residential services for the mentally retarded. Washington D. C.: President's Committee on Mental Retardation, 1969(a).

Blatt, B. Recommendations for the institutional reform. In R. Kugel & W. Wolfensberger (Eds.), Changing patterns in residential services for the mentally retarded. Washington, D. C.: President's Committee on Mental Retardation, 1969(b).

Blatt, B. Empty revolution beyond the mental. In F. Menolascino (Ed.), Psychiatric approaches to mental retardation. New York: Basic Books, 1970.

Dewey, J. Theory of valuation. Chicago: Univ. of Chicago Press, 1939.

Gardner, J. M. Innovation in the delivery of psychological services in an institution. American Psychologist, 1971, 26, 211-214.

Keith, K. D. Analysis of institutional staff behavior. Mental Retardation, 1972, 10, 44-45.

Miller, G. On turning psychology over to the unwashed. Psychology Today, 1969, 3, 53-54, 66-74.

Nirje, B. A Scandinavian visitor looks at U.S. institutions. In R. Kugel & W. Wolfensberger (Eds.), Changing patterns in residential services for the mentally retarded. Washington, D. C.: President's Committee on Mental Retardation, 1969.

Odiorne, G. S. Management by objectives. New York: Pitman, 1965.

Panyan, M., Boozer, H., & Morris, N. Feedback to attendants as a reinforcer for applying operant techniques. Journal of Applied Behavior Analysis, 1970, 3, 1-4.

Roos, P. Evolutionary changes of the residential facility. In A. Baumeister & E. Butterfield (Eds.), Residential facilities for the mentally retarded. Chicago: Aldine, 1970.

Rosenthal, R. Experimenter effects in behavioral research. New York: Appleton-Century-Crofts, 1966.

Sage, H. M. Interim report regarding a study of programming impediments: Part II of three parts. Beatrice, Nebr.: Beatrice State Home Library, 1972.

Schaefer, H. M. & Martin, P. L. Behavioral Therapy. New York: McGraw-Hill, 1969.

Shafter, A. J. A philosophy of administration: A revisit. Mental Retardation, 1971, 9(5), 3-5.

Skinner, B. F. Beyond freedom and dignity. New York: Alfred A. Knopf, 1971.

Watson, L. S. Behavior modification of residents and personnel in institutions for the mentally retarded. In A. Baumeister & E. Butterfield (Eds.), Residential facilities for the mentally retarded. Chicago: Aldine, 1970.

Watson, L. S., Gardner, J. M., & Sanders, C. Shaping and maintaining behavior modification skills in staff members in an MR institution: Columbus State Institute behavior modification program. Mental Retardation, 1971, 9(3), 39-42.

Wolfensberger, W. The origin and nature of our institutional models. In R. Kugel & W. Wolfensberger (Eds.), Changing patterns in residential services for the mentally retarded. Washington, D. C.: President's Committee on Mental Retardation, 1969.

Wolfensberger, W. Will there always be an institution? I: The impact of epidemiological trends. Mental Retardation, 1971, 9, 14-20.

THE UNIVERSITY-AFFILIATED FACILITY
Paul H. Pearson

The words "University - Affiliated Facility" or Center relate to a specific program concept which had its origins in federal legislation passed during those incomparable - at least for mental retardation - days of the Kennedy era. Title I, Part B, of P. L. 88-164, as later amended by P. L. 90-170 authorized construction grants to institutions of higher learning for interdisciplinary training of specialized and generic personnel needed to provide quality services to the mentally retarded. A total of nineteen construction grants were awarded at a total cost in excess of $77, 900, 000 of which $41, 836, 000 were federal funds. Five grants were for multiple buildings at different campus locations for a total of twenty-five buildings. An additional UAF was constructed with funds provided under Title I, Part A, of P. L. 88-164 for an overall total of twenty centers. (See list of UAF centers.)

These facilities were to demonstrate the provisions of a full range of specialized services for persons with mental retardation and provide the interdisciplinary training of personnel needed for research, diagnosis and treatment, education, training, and habilitation or care of persons with mental retardation.

UNIVERSITY-AFFILIATED FACILITIES

Region I
Children's Hospital Medical Center
Boston, Massachusetts 02115

Walter E. Fernald State School
Waltham, Massachusetts 02154

Region III
Georgetown University
Washington, D. C. 20007

Johns Hopkins
Baltimore, Maryland 21205

Temple University
Philadelphia, Pennsylvania 19122

Region V
Indiana University (Bloomington)
Bloomington, Indiana 47401

Indiana University (Indianapolis)
Indianapolis, Indiana 46207

The University of Michigan
Ann Arbor, Michigan 48104

University of Cincinnati
Cincinnati, Ohio 45220

Ohio State University
Columbus, Ohio 43210

University of Wisconsin
Madison, Wisconsin 53706

Region VII
University of Iowa
Iowa City, Iowa 52240

University of Nebraska Medical Center
Omaha, Nebraska 68106

University of Kansas (Lawrence)
Lawrence, Kansas 66103

University of Kansas (Parsons)
Parsons, Kansas 67357

St. Louis University
St. Louis, Missouri 63104

University of Missouri
Columbia, Missouri 65201

Region II
Newark State College
Union, New Jersey 07083

Albert Einstein College of Medicine
Bronx, New York 10461

New York Medical College
New York, New York 10595

Region IV
University of Alabama (Birmingham)
Birmingham, Alabama 35486

University of Alabama (Tuscaloosa)
Tuscaloosa, Alabama 35486

University of Miami
Miami, Florida 33152

Georgia Retardation Center (Atlanta)
Atlanta, Georgia 30341

Georgia Retardation Center (Athens)
Athens, Georgia 30601

University of North Carolina
Chapel Hill, North Carolina 27514

University of Tennessee
Memphis, Tennessee 38105

Region VI
Louisiana State University
New Orleans, Louisiana 70112

Region VIII
University of South Dakota
Vermillion, South Dakota 57069

Utah State University
Logan, Utah 84321

Region IX
University of California (Los Angeles)
Los Angeles, California 90024

University of California (Irvine)
Irvine, California 92664

Region X
University of Oregon (Eugene)
Eugene, Oregon 97403

University of Oregon (Portland)
Portland, Oregon 97201

University of Washington (Seattle)
Seattle, Washington 98195

Compiled 1972

In 1970, the Congress further amended P. L. 88-164 with the passage of P. L. 91-157, the Developmental Disabilities Services and Facilities Construction Act. This law not only expanded the focus from mental retardation to include other developmental disabilities needing similar services to the mentally retarded but for the first time authorized grants for administering and operating the UAF program. These funds were authorized under Title II of the Act and are distinct from those funds awarded to the states under Title I, the state formula grant for planning, administration, services and construction of facilities for the developmentally disabled. "Seed grants" were awarded to twelve centers not constructed under the P. L. 88-164 construction grants but which had developed according to the criteria for University - Affiliated Facilities, while support grants were made to those 25 centers constructed under P. L. 88-164.

No funding, however, was authorized for either the educational or service programs. Support for these functions must be obtained from a variety of federal, state and local sources. The Maternal and Child Health Service, H. S. M. H. A., under

Section 511 of the Social Security Act has supported training for health service personnel related to the care of children at most of the centers constructed under P. L. 88-164. However, these funds have been totally committed and are not now available to the emerging UAF's.

As the name indicates, these centers were to be university based, but integrated into the community service system with the freedom or, perhaps more accurately the requirement that they provide training for students not just from within their own campus but rather from any school or training program within their region. In other words, other schools could "affiliate" with the university center so as to obtain for their students specific experience in an interdisciplinary center. Training was to be provided for both professionals and direct care personnel. For example, it is mandatory for each center in order to be eligible for federal support to have a cooperative training program with a junior college or, as in Nebraska's case, a community college; thus insuring that not only will the university be training the Ph. D. 's and M. D. 's for teaching and research careers but the technicians and specialists to provide skilled, direct personal care as well.

The federal guidelines for University - Affiliated Facilities clearly indicate that these centers are to exemplify the principles and practices which will lead to increasingly effective programs of prevention, treatment and habilitation, including participation in planning activities. While the usual resources of the University are expected to provide the basic elements, the center is not to limit its activities and concerns to the academic setting only, but must involve itself in all appropriate ways with the special needs and resources of the community and region within which it operates.

The training program must provide a wide range of training opportunities including both graduate and undergraduate programs, full time practicum courses, short term workshops, general orientation experiences, etc. Not only must the interdisciplinary training be offered to those people who will "specialize" but also to those who should be knowledgeable about the field when they come across specific problems within their daily work. Included in the latter category are such diverse fields as probation officers, legislators, guidance counselors, architects, planners, ministers, etc.

The centers are required to remain responsive to the service needs of the developmentally disabled and must maintain a continuous and close relationship with the State Developmental Disabilities Planning and Advisory Councils within the region served by the center. Technical assistance is to be provided not only to the Councils but to other agencies both state and local, regarding programming, administrative methods, teaching methods, and special problems such as legal questions, space utilization, etc. Dissemination of information concerning developmental disabilities is also expected from the UAF.

Research objectives of the center are to be commensurate with the training objectives. In addition, the center should be involved in the development of data regarding service and manpower needs, means of evaluating programs - both training and service - as well as clinical information about the clients served. These research findings should then be disseminated and fed back into the service and training program so as to continually improve them.

The "reason for being" of University - Affiliated Facilities, then, is as interdisciplinary training centers. Why interdisciplinary instead of the more standard departmentalized or even multi-disciplinary training programs of our schools and universities? The answer lies in the fact that traditional departmentalized training does not prepare the professional to interact with the many different disciplines required in the wide spectrum of services needed by the developmentally disabled. One writer referred to public and voluntary agencies as "circumscribed islands of service". They might have gone one step further to say that these circumscribed islands were separated by oceans of professional mistrust and misunderstandings, oceans that were buffeted by the strong winds of professionalism and dotted by the high reefs of discipline domains.

The major cause for all of this interprofessional difficulty and certainly the largest barrier to successful collaboration is simply one of communication between the professions and the resulting lack of understanding of each other's objectives and concerns, or of the unique contribution that the other professions can make to a particular case. Quite obviously, the best time to develop this understanding and ability to communicate between the professions is that point in training when the trainee begins to apply his knowledge, that is during the practicum or field work training. Since it is at this time that the student acquire the principles under which he will probably work the rest of his career, it seems equally obvious that unless he is exposed to a model of interprofessional coordination and collaboration at this time, it will be much more difficult for him to learn the necessary principles and means of communication at a later date.

I think the previous presentations have underlined at least

two more good reasons for interdisciplinary education and training; first, the problem of the improperly trained professional or one whose attitude is wrong and secondly, the essential need to have the skills of the various professionals literally merge around the developmentally disabled individual if we are going to provide the proper management for his complex problems. The latter point has the most relevance for UAF's but the first is equally important.

It might be easy to gain the impression from some of the things said by the previous speakers that we do not really need highly trained people working in programs for the mentally retarded, that is, all we really need is love. I said it might be easy to get that idea, except that obviously all the previous speakers are very highly trained individuals themselves. What I heard was that there are very serious dangers in improperly trained professionals or with any personnel who have the wrong concepts and attitudes.

If I had to point to one basic problem from the situations described earlier, I would have to say that it arises from the tendency on the part of many professionals to label the child rather than labeling the services to be utilized by the individual. The dangers arising from doing this were first pointed out to me some years ago by Gunnar Dybwad. Labels lead to generalizations and as Dybwad has said, "We have been far too much influenced by prejudicial generalization as to the expected learning capacity of mentally retarded persons in general and have let these generali - zations stand in the way of needed efforts to assist each of these individuals towards his highest possible level of life fulfillment at home, at work, and at play. "

In other words, we make our diagnosis become a prognosis. If we label the child as a "trainable retardate", we are not likely to consider whether or not he might possibly be capable of moving into a class for the educable retarded after some specific training. On the other hand, if instead of labeling the child, we describe his particular abilities at a particular point in time and describe the proper program for him, we leave open the possibility that he may well exceed our expectation and be able to move up into a higher functioning level. Johnny, who tests out at the moment as a high level moderately retarded child and therefore eligible for a <u>class</u> for the trainable retarded may quite possibly be able to move up into a <u>class</u> for the educable retarded if he is highly motivated and receives the proper special education. Even the label "retarded" needs to be used with care since we have seen too many multiply handicapped children who at a very young age tested as function- ally retarded but who after attendance in our early education pro- gram or after serious physical handicaps have been ameliorated are able to function in the normal range of intelligence and move on into regular classrooms.

The need to have the skills of the various professionals literally merge around the developmentally disabled individual is well illustrated in Una Haynes' presentation of the cross modality approach. The point here is that the professional must work closely with others in order to best apply his own professional skills in working with the child with multiple handicaps. This is particularly applicable when dealing with infants and very young children where only one therapist may carry out treatment recommendations for the child. The physical therapist or the occupational therapist in the developmental disabilities must function as teachers of motor skills so they must be knowledgeable about techniques of reinforcement, the importance of motivation and attention, of effort, the need for repetition, and must learn to deal with the hyperactive child and the problem of short attention span.

The teacher, the speech therapist and the psychologist must be aware of how the motor difficulties of the child with cerebral palsy directly effects their effort. They must know how to deal with asymmetric tonic neck reflex, how to position the child with spastic or athetoid cerebral palsy so as to reduce abnormal muscle tone, and maximize the child's ability to attend to stimuli other than his own internal ones. The teacher or the speech pathologist must learn how to free the vocal muscles and/or the upper extremity muscles from the abnormal impulses that interfere with proper vocalization and hand skills. The psychologist is not the only one who needs to know about Piaget. The physical therapist and the occupational therapist who have at least a practical understanding of the need for integration of experience between sensory modalities will undoubtedly be better able to utilize the neuromotor techniques taught by the Bobaths.

In other words, the child is a whole and can only interact with one professional at a time. The professional must be prepared to cope with the child's total disabilities at least to the extent that they directly affect his own efforts.

One of the best articles that I have come across discussing interdisciplinary efforts is a paper by Dr. George Szasz, Assistant Professor of Health Care and Epidemiology on the faculty of medicine at the University of British Columbia, Vancouver, British Columbia. Dr. Szasz makes the previously stated points that communication among those providing comprehensive services needs to be improved and that if professionals are to work together they must learn together. The problem, he says, is to determine what students need to learn together and how they should learn it. The difficulties that arise usually result from vagueness of objectives, lack of role models, inflexible time tables, conservatism, distrust between professions, and failure to perceive emerging needs. He lists the following barriers that exist between the professions: social or psychological differences, economic differences, technological differences, and status differences. These disparities are often reflected in differences in income, enthusiasm, and motivation.

He goes on to point out "a basic problem inherent in traditional education also contributes to the establishment of barriers. Traditionally, education in western societies has stressed competitive, non-cooperative principles." He gives as examples the grades given to students and the academic rewards which come down through departmental channels with a very limited room at the top. There are few, if any, role models in professional schools that offer examples of the principles of cooperation.

Thus, it should be clear that the concept behind the University-Affiliated Facility is a challenging one to implement. It must develop and evolve from within a basically antagonistic system -- the departmentally structured university. Their own internal structure, if it is to provide the interdisciplinary role model for students, must de-emphasize many traditional professional relationships. Many well motivated but traditionally trained faculty members are unable to make this necessary adjustment. Often there are conflicting demands on their time and loyalty between their academic department and the University-Affiliated Facility.

Many university faculty members are reluctant to venture out of their "ivory tower" to work in the "real world" - a reluctance often at least partially justified on the basis of previous unpleasant or unproductive experiences. Further stress is placed on the UAF's staff when they must attempt to reconcile the objectives required by the university that employs them with those arising from the priorities of the State Planning and Advisory Council for the Developmental Disabilities or with those community agencies with whom they are trying to cooperate. When this is further extended to regional responsibilities, the permutations and combinations for differing needs, objectives, and plain misunderstanding become immense.

Despite these at times staggering difficulties, the University-Affiliated Facilities appear to be gaining adherence both within the universities and within their communities of action, although they have yet to demonstrate the validity of their conceptual base due to a combination of under funding and their short tenure. Undoubtedly they must do this to justify their continued public support. Achievement of this goal, however, will depend as much on the cooperation and understanding of those people and agencies with whom they must interact as it will on the ingenuity and stamina of the University - Affiliated Facility leadership.

To summarize my above remarks I would say that the essence of the University - Affiliated Facility is that it must be a bridge between research or the development of new knowledge, education or manpower development, and the development of exemplary community services. It also has to be a bridge between the departments within the University itself. Anyone who has ever worked within the University system knows how difficult it is to break down the walls of departmentalization with its rigid parochial system of rewards. We must break down these walls, enlarge professional outlook, and bring about an increasing awareness of the need for a comprehensive approach to the broad spectrum of human problems in the developmental disabilities - knowledge of the aids available from members of other professions, and an understanding of attitudes, values and methods of those providing these aids. Further, the UAF must serve as a bridge between the

168

University and the community wherein lie the long time problems of "town and gown". In other words, the UAF should also serve as a bridge between the "circumscribed islands" of community services.

And last, but far from the least, they can serve as another bridge into the promised land of normalization and equality of developmental opportunity for the developmentally disabled.

REFERENCES

Dybwad, G. Who are the mentally retarded? Presentation made at the Summer Institute on Social Work in the Rehabilitation of Mentally Retarded Persons, at Teachers College-Columbia University, New York City, July, 1967.

Fierber, N. M. & Kliewer, D. Physical therapy in a children's rehabilitation center. In P. H. Pearson and C. E. Williams (Eds.) Physical therapy services in the developmental disabilities. Springfield, Illinois: C. C. Thomas, 1972.

Halpern, D. Rehabilitation therapy in support of education of multiply-handicapped children. Unpublished manuscript, University of Minnesota, Department of Physical Medicine and Rehabilitation, 1971.

Swasz, G. Interprofessional education in the health sciences. Milbank Memorial Fund Quarterly, 1969, 47, 449-475.

PARENTS OF THE MENTALLY RETARDED

Introduction (Editors)

This portion of the Conference focused on two key aspects of working effectively with parents of the retarded: 1) Understanding their personal-family needs and finding effective routes for helping them to help their child (regardless of his level and/or type of retardation); and 2) An overview of the major current challenges of the National Association for Retarded Children—the major advocate group on behalf of retarded citizens in the United States, as they relate to the provision of services for the severely and profoundly retarded. Each of these two parental dimensions of mental retardation is presented in its own right as separate presentations.

UNDERSTANDING PARENTS OF THE RETARDED—A CRISIS MODEL FOR HELPING THEM COPE MORE EFFECTIVELY
Frank J. Menolascino

I plan to review some differential patterns of family interaction and management in the area of mental retardation. Included are the frequently encountered issues from the initial
entry into the family attitudes concerning their child -- to
treatment approaches that enlist their cooperation in initiating
an empathic and energetic program aimed at fulfilling their child's
developmental potentials. The stages of parental acceptance
that are relevant to current management approaches will initially
be reviewed, and then an operational framework which extends
this approach into a crisis oriented approach which embraces
both diagnostic and specific treatment guidelines. I shall stress
that the rewards of successful management far outweigh the additional efforts that are frequently necessary in regard to professional involvement and time. Indeed, successful initial assessment and management of these family attitudes and problems may
avoid institutionalization by default -- especially in parents of
severely and/or profoundly retarded children.

Stages of Parental Acceptance

It has become clear to clinicians in the field of mental retardation that the initial interpretation interview is a cornerstone
for the future act of implementation of treatment - management
recommendations for any given child and his parents. If we fail
to help the parents understand their child's problems -- we may
well be sending them further on the path of "carrousel medicine,"
or what has been termed "shopping patterns" for further diagnostic services, rather than effective treatment intervention.
The initial interpretation interview is thus crucial to all further
treatment and habilitation attempts. However, the practice of
diagnostic interpretation and parental counseling in the area of
mental retardation is a most demanding one, and the clinician
who embarks on such a course needs certain skills in order to
be effective (Solomons, 1970). Among these skills are: 1) Knowledge of the disease states or syndromes which can produce mental
retardation as one of the symptoms. Such knowledge allows the
clinician to share his diagnostic conclusions with the parents
without feeling uneasy with terms, findings, or parental questions
as to prognostic implications. 2) He must be able to explain and
discuss diagnostic findings in a manner that is in keeping with
the parental level of understanding -- both intellectually and
emotionally. Here we must avoid the tactic of many parents to

attribute all of their child's clinical picture to some "organic"

entity in an effort to relieve any self-guilt and/or perplexity

concerning same. The initial diagnostic interpretation to parents

who do not even suspect mental retardation (e.g., the initial

shock of Down's syndrome) will be totally ineffective unless

the emotional reactions of the parents are anticipated and handled

before firm diagnostic statements are made -- or the diagnosis

may come like a "bolt out of the sky." 3) An intimate under-

standing of the family dynamics (being obtained from a previous

review of the family dynamics which includes their marital inter-

actional patterns, the nature of the support system as to the

extended family, etc.) is necessary in order to know when and how

much to interpret. The initial interpretation interview is an

extremely important step. For example, in 22 percent of the

children seen in our initial sample of 616 cases (Menolascino,

1965), the parents had already either known or strongly suspected

that their child was mentally retarded. Thus the proper sensitive

management of the initial interview with this particular group of

parents led to emotional abreaction of a sufficient quantity to

produce a stage of acceptance of their child's disabilities and

then rapid movement toward realistic treatment programming

for the child. It was in the other 78 percent of our parent group that we noted mechanisms that have been well delineated in the clinical literature as stages of parental reaction and acceptance or rejection of the diagnosis of mental retardation.

The stages of parental acceptance can be briefly reviewed as follows: 1) The parents may not have fully accepted the diagnosis of mental retardation in their child and here one frequently notes: a) <u>Shock</u> -- "It can't be true," or "How can they tell?", or "What did we do to deserve this?" (strong religious overtones are common), and b) <u>Denial</u> -- "He is just a little slow" (with inappropriate and seemingly endless "catching up" fantasies). Unsuccessful intervention and management of either of these two parental responses can lead to further medical shopping for "the" diagnosis. 2) The parents may have varying degrees of <u>guilt</u> feelings about their own possible roles in the causation of the child's condition. This usually presents itself clinically as the mother worrying unduly about, "The bad fall I had--", inference statements such as, "My wife has some rather strange people in her family tree--", or more direct attempts to displace their perceived guilt by side stepping and/or resenting the reality fact -- followed by energetic efforts to find some external family source onto which they can project the problem. Favorite targets of and for projection here are the family doctor (i.e., delivery, instruments, vague febrile episodes that were "inadequately treated", etc.). The lack of intervention at this point can lead to increasingly more pathological coping devices as manifest by an obsessive search for "magical" solutions (Wolfensberger & Menolascino, 1970). In the older child, derogative comments concerning local special educational facilities and negative expectations therefrom are frequent. Accordingly, failure of successful therapeutic intervention at this point rapidly leads toward the use of more primitive defense mechanisms -- both individually on the part of each parent, and collectively in regard to the family's approach to their child's problems and needs. Overly aggressive, almost paranoid, coping devices come to the foreground, and a very strong undercurrent of depression is frequently apparent in each or both of the parents. One notes a shift from direct focus on the child's needs, to unsuccessful attempts on the part of both parents to quell their internal turmoil. 3) A similar parental response is one in which a reaction formation is utilized as a thin veneer to solve their unconscious wishes to rid themselves of the burden that they begin to view their child as representing to both their personal needs and ability to handle or control the situation. The reaction formation type of defense is usually manifested clinically

176

by overaction and/or over-compensations in the form of excessive protection and concern about the child, or by aggressively demanding special and additional attention for their child. At this point, the previously noted shopping for diagnostic labels tends to slowly change to therapeutic shopping (i.e., "Is he not mentally retarded -- but perhaps an autistic or schizophrenic child?"). Herein we frequently see a shift from the denial of the child's developmental problems towards a vague position on causation (e.g., "Damage to his brain") on which they can project the "reasons" of the child's developmental problems. The request for inappropriate treatment at this time literally spells out the irrational (unconscious) nature of their reaction to the child's problems (i.e., distortion of the external reality referents of their child's developmental problems into a paradigm which so structures the situation that they themselves can also obtain professional services.).

In summary, the initial multi-disciplinary diagnostic evaluation of the child and his family must include an assessment of the stage the family is at as to their knowledge of the nature of his problems, acceptance of their child's problems, and their willingness to cooperate in a mutual treatment approach. With

177

this type of overall orientation, then the interpretation interview can quickly zero in on where the parents are in their working with and working out their own emotional responses to their child. Thus, with thorough initial assessment of the nature of the parent's stage of acceptance of their child's problems, one can move toward differential management considerations that focus on family counseling and/or guidance.

It is important to realize that parental guilt is common in these areas. Since the parents conceived the child, they feel responsible for any difficulties he may have, just as they would take pride in a gifted child (similarly, parents of emotionally disturbed children present a different mechanism of managing the guilt factors that are present.). Unlike the emotionally disturbed child, the parents of a mentally retarded child can't really project their guilt (e.g., onto school authorities, etc.) since the ultimate projection must be onto themselves. This has particular relevance to the crisis of personal values that I will discuss shortly.

Evolution of a Crisis Orientation to Diagnosis and Management of Parents of the Retarded

I have reviewed some general professional guidelines toward parents of the mentally retarded. Before presenting some specific guidelines -- I would like to place the remarks in perspective.

In scanning the early literature on mental retardation, one is struck by the fact that very little mention was made of parents, of their feelings, or the impact of the diagnosis upon them. In the mid-1940's through the early 1950's, a trickle of armchair papers began to discuss the relevant parent dynamics, to be followed by almost a flood of such papers in the more recent past. It is also curious to note that the parents discussed in the literature are rarely representative of parents of the retarded in general. Instead, they often tend to be 1) Mothers; 2) of middle and upper class status; 3) White; and 4) Consumers of outpatient diagnostic clinic services. Nevertheless, generalizations are only too readily drawn about parents of the retarded. Failure to include fathers in research, over-reliance on maternal information and an assumption that such maternal information, particularly regarding the father, is valid are very common. In regards to the latter, Ross (1964) has noted, "Reading the scientific literature in this field, a student unfamiliar with our culture might easily get the impression that fathers play no part in the rearing of our children."

Many writers who comment upon parents' initial reactions to learning that their child is retarded are actually only referring to a minority among parents. The parents who have provided the "case material" for many writers were disproportionately middle and upper-class parents of lower functioning children and this has probably introduced some bias. In only a very small number of children can the diagnosis be made at birth. In the vast majority of cases, diagnosis is made at school age, and if mild retardation is, indeed, already of concern to such parents, awareness of its existence usually grows gradually and does not have the sudden impact as often implied in the literature. Even in severe and profoundly retarded children the diagnosis usually arises out of the observation of retarded development. More often than not formal diagnosis only confirm the parents' apprehensions, and while the act of confirmation may be abrupt and sudden, the suspicion or even knowledge of retardation may have been present for months or years.

A Review of Parental Management Approaches

Early conceptualizations of parental response to a retarded child were heavily influenced by psychoanalytic thought. Major emphasis was placed on the role of guilt, which was seen as a near-universal phenomenon in parents of all types of handicapped children. These parents were commonly viewed as conflicted and almost certain to engage in defense mechanisms such as denial and projection, and it was expected that such defenses would be

180

of neurotic proportions. Virtually, everything the parent did was interpreted as constituting "rejection" or "non-acceptance" of the child, and parental behavior that had positive elements was, at worst, labeled as reaction formation or, at best, as ambivalence. The psychoanalytic interpretation reached its apex with two elaborations. One of these was by Beddie and Osmond (1955) who equated parental response to a retarded child as equivalent to a "child loss" (death of a normal child) resulting in grief that required "grief work" in order to be overcome. Institutionalization was seen as a "death without the proper rites." The other elaboration, by Solnit and Stark (1961), coined the term "chronic mourning" for the "object loss" to which the advent of the retarded child was equated. This grief motif became widely accepted and management approaches which flowed from these psychoanalytic concepts tended to incorporate several elements: (1) The parent was placed into the role of a psychiatric patient, which the parent was expected to accept if he was to be helped. (2) Help consisted primarily of therapeutically oriented individual or group counseling which explored the parent's feelings about his own parents, as well as about the child and his condition and problems. (3) The parent was encouraged to express his deep-seated feelings of responsibility for the child's condition and was provided interpretation, reassurance, and support in an effort to dissipate guilt. Usually, management did not go much beyond this because, on the one hand, parents were now assumed to be able to make the best adjustment possible under the circumstances and, on the other hand, there prevailed a very pessimistic -- almost nihilistic -- view about treatment horizons for the retarded child. Thus, there seemed to be little to do in a concrete way except perhaps to recommend institutional placement and to make the necessary arrangements for same.

More recently, stress has been placed on the realistic demands and burdens that parents of retarded children often bear. Parents were seen as being under a great deal of situational and external stress, and symptoms of such stress were perceived as essentially normal or at least expected under the circumstances. The neurotic interpretation of parental reactions was specifically attacked and rejected by Olshansky (1962, 1966). He pointed to certain social factors of our culture which induce parents to feel devalued for having a damaged child and to other co-existing factors which inhibit his ability to externalize this sorrow so as to dissipate it. Such a conflict was seen as apt to result in long-term internalization of a depressive mood which Olshansky termed "chronic sorrow" as an understandable non-neurotic response to a tragic fact. The management suggested by Olshansky emphasized ventilation of parental feelings, readiness on the part of the professional to act scapegoat - like as a focus of anger to the parent, and provision of concrete services such as nursery schools, special classes, sheltered workshops, and guidance with practical problems of child rearing.

Farber (1959) advanced a sociological and relatively sophisticated theory of parental response to a retarded child. Briefly, parental conflicts were seen to spring from two types of "crisis" situations: a "tragic crisis" occurs when parents are unable to cope with a retarded child over a long period of time. This theory has given rise to a number of studies by Farber, his students, and others, but since the main interest in this work has been theoretical, there has been little elaboration in regard to management implications.

A NEW MANAGEMENT FRAMEWORK

Each of the conceptualizations which have been briefly reviewed has made some contribution toward a better understanding of families of the retarded. However, the approaches have suffered from emphasizing only limited aspects of either the problem or the possible management options. I will attempt to unify some of the thinking and to propose a framework that we have found helpful in handling a wide variety of problems and situations, and that may provide a means for a more judicious selection of management options.

It is proposed that parental management needs arising from the advent or presence of a retarded child tend to have three major sources: novelty shock, which results when parental expectancies are suddenly shattered; value conflicts due to culturally mediated attitudes toward defect or deviance; reality stress resulting from the situational demands of raising or caring for a retarded person. Each of these sources will be discussed in detail below.

The Novelty Shock Crisis

Novelty shock is very natural response that occurs when parents learn precipitously that their expectations and perceptions in regard to their child deviate substantially from reality. Novelty shock may occur when a parent of an older child learns relatively suddenly that the child is or may be retarded. However, most commonly, novelty shock occurs upon the birth of an obviously atypical child, such as a child with Down's Syndrome.

Parents usually have great anticipations as to what the prospective baby may be like. Most immediately, there are certain basic normative expectations as to size and weight and that the baby will have similar racial characteristics as the parents. Aside from these basic normative characteristics, parents -- especially if they have not had children before -- are apt to idealize the expected baby. As Solnit and Stark (1961) have stated so well, parents often do not merely expect a typical infant but a perfect one. Aside from expectations as to the qualities of their baby, parents have expectations in regard to the future. In our culture, most parents strongly expect their children to pursue an education, to marry, and to practice an occupation. Some parents not only establish college education funds for children that are not even born yet, but they may even have picked -- at least in their fantasies -- the college their child is to attend and the occupation he is to assume.

The time of birth itself is, under the best of circumstances, a time of severe physical and emotional stress for both mother and father, accompanied by uncertainty and emotionality. Any additional stressful events superimposed on such a state of vulnerability and depletion are apt to cause bewilderment, confusion, disorganization, regression to increased dependency upon others, and may be even temporary psychosis. Obviously, an unexpected and stressful event associated with the occasion itself, such as the birth of a grossly atypical child, is particularly apt to induce such a state, conceptualized here as novelty shock. Actually, the fact that the child is damaged and likely to be retarded may not be the critical issue. The general disruption of expectancies may be more traumatic than the specific nature of the reality. For illustration's sake, we might say that novelty shock might be equally severe whether the baby is diagnosed as Down's Syndrome, or whether it is 3 feet long, very premature, has purple horns of unexpected racial characteristics, whether it is healthy but dies unexpectedly, or whether the baby turned out to be more than one baby. Often it is not even the unexpected event that induces shock as much as the way the event is interpreted by all involved, including the medical personnel. Imagine an authoritarian medical figure towering over a depleted, lonely, perhaps half-conscious mother, booming dramatically: "Madam, you have just given birth to a mongolian idiot who should be institutionalized immediately!" Incidents of this nature have by no means been rare and are well documented in the literature (for example, Aldrich, 1947; Holt, 1958; Tizard and Grad, 1961; Zwerling, 1954; Waskowitz, 1959).

The literature also documents that parents can go into novelty shock merely on the basis of the awareness that some terrible event has happened even when they lack all understanding of the terminology that is thrown at them or of the nature of meaning of the event. McDonald (1962) documented a case where a father walked the streets in confused agitation for two nights and a day after being told that his baby had a cleft palate; he came back asking what a cleft palate was. Kramm (1963) told of a mother who was informed that her child was a mongoloid and who set out with the help of neighbors and dictionaries to find out what a mongoloid was, eventually concluding that it was something kindred to a mongrel dog. Other parents have been known to have been kept from seeing their child or to have been induced into not wanting to see it. One such family finally came in fear and apprehension to see their institutionalized baby which, on the basis of the guidance they had received, they had pictured as an unspeakable monster -- and instead found a sweet, beautiful mongoloid baby that they would probably have taken home loved, and raised if there had been better interpretation earlier.

It is apparent that management for novelty shock must often undo the damage wrought by others who were on the scene earlier. What parents in novelty shock need first and foremost is gentle, undramatic interpretation of the facts, provided in an atmosphere of maximal emotional support. Reading matter and audio-visual devices might be highly useful Also, interpretation should stress those elements which are realistically positive, such as the positive aspects of likely child development and the availability or expected availability of services and resources. To cope with their grief, parents should be helped to get to know fellow parents (i. e. , "Pilot parents" from local Associations for Retarded Children) who have experienced similar traumas and who have made model adjustments. Where a newborn baby is involved, management should not terminate when the mother leaves the hospital but should continue as needed.

In order to be able to provide facts and information to the parents, it is necessary to assess the condition of the child. However, a comprehensive assessment may be neither possible nor desirable at that time: on the other hand, since parental novelty shock occurs almost invariably either at the child's birth or during the first years, one must postpone many judgments until one has had the opportunity to see the child respond to environmental conditions and services. Thus, it is important to incorporate into the fact-oriented management approach a reasonable balance of caution, uncertainty, and positive elements. Assessment of the child should not attempt to attain a certainty that is not attainable at that time; instead, assessment must be viewed and interpreted as a time-bound process. Such emphasis upon the uncertainty of the future should not be mistaken as merely a device for softening the emotional impact upon the parents; uncertainty is valid even in some very clear-cut and relatively homogeneous syndromes such as Down's and others where occasionally remarkable deviations from typical syndromic expressions may occur. The benefits of an early, sudden, and somewhat dramatic diagnosis appear to have been greatly exaggerated. Such a "diagnosis-compulsion" on the part of the manager may often be detrimental rather than beneficial (Wolfensberger, 1965).

It appears that parents in novelty shock tend to become very inward-directed, usually in a selfish and self-pitying manner. Successful adaptation often requires that the parent broaden his concerns to the spouse and the child. Thus, management that emphasizes future assessment of the child's progress can help the parent to move from a helpless, disordered dependency to a more adaptive concern about maximizing the child's development. One might say that it is better for the parent to move toward a reality stress situation than to remain in novelty shock.

The novelty shock reaction is likely to be well circumscribed and definable, and the management implications tend to be rather clear. However, such reactions -- though perhaps memorable because of the extremity of parental response -- are relatively rare. In a few instances, an unexpectedly atypical child is born and recognized at birth. In a few other cases, a child is suddenly recognized as significantly atypical sometime after birth. But in the vast majority of cases, recognition comes mercifully slow or some events prior to or associated with pregnancy have sensitized the parent to the possibility that the infant may be atypical.

The Reality Stress Crisis

Even to rear a child that is gifted, healthy, and beautiful is a tremendously demanding task, and we can see everywhere in the world around us how easy it is for relatively normal adults to fail in the task of rearing children who initially at least were rather typical infants. Therefore it must be underscored that the task of rearing an atypical child is very likely to constitute such a demand that typical parents cannot be expected to manage adequately without being provided with extraordinary resources and services.

It is to be expected that parents of retarded children will increasingly present themselves to psychiatrists and agencies such as psychiatric clinics in search of help. While the parents may display signs of stress and occasionally even psychopath-ology, we must recognize that such symptoms may be no more than normative reactions to situational stress. It is important to realize that crises or conflicts due to excessive reality demands are essentially normal and are only to a limited degree under the control of the parents. Psychiatric management of families of the retarded has sometimes ignored the realistic burdens associated with rearing an atypical child and instead has tended to be preoccupied with parental psychopathology. Indeed, in the literature one can find endless examples where parents are stereotyped as guilty, rejecting, unaccepting, where they are viewed as "the patient," and where excessive faith is placed on therapeutically oriented counseling rather than on education or provision of concrete relief measures. The physical demands made by a hyperactive child can rarely be handled by counseling alone, and the demands of caring for three children still in diapers are not lightened by probing the mother's anal fixations and deep-seated feelings about feces. If any kind of counseling for such a mother is appropriate, it is of the type that introduces her to operant behavior shaping, but a didactic approach accompanied by home visits would probably be optional.

All professionals who participate in the management of families of the retarded should be sensitive to the temptation to provide management that might be provided better by others. Instead of maintaining management dominance while doing something that they have been trained to do but that is irrelevant in the specific case, a professional would do better to act as an effective advocate or aggressive referral and follow-up agent in seeing to it that somebody will provide the management that is appropriate and needed in a given case.

Measures of major and most poignant relevance to the relief of reality stress are the following: concrete and direct services, such as obtaining acceptance of a child in a day-care or special education program or inclusion of an adult in a vocational training or sheltered-work program; seeing to it that home-maker, visiting nurse, or home economist services are initiated; getting the family enrolled in appropriate clinics and health services; initiating casework to obtain public assistance for which the family may be eligible; exercising advocacy functions to safeguard rights and prevent exploitation, especially of the poor and disadvantaged; providing the family with education in regard to problems of child care, especially feeding, dressing, and toileting the handicapped child; providing the family with equipment (perhaps on a loan basis) that facilitates child care

or accelerates child development, for example, walkers, stand-

ing tables, toilet chairs, feeding aides; helping find competent

baby sitters; assisting in arrangements for residential placement;

and so on.

Value Conflicts

Clinicians tend to be more adept at tracing individual psy-

chopathology to pathogenic events and patterns in persons' back-

grounds -- than in dealing with the powerful effects of social and

subcultural values and attitudes which are transmitted in rela-

tively "normal" fashion and which may rule a person's behavior.

In our society, there are many perceptions and interpretations

of mental retardation that have been transmitted to us from the

past. We must recall that, by definition, retardation is a devi-

ancy. In other words, retarded persons are significantly differ-

ent from others, and in our society the difference is generally

negatively valued. Thus, common historical role perceptions

of the retardate have included the retardate as a menace, as

subhuman (animal-like or even vegetative), as an objective of

ridicule, and as an object of pity (Wolfensberger, 1969a). Some

role perceptions have been more common in some of our sub-

cultures than others. For instance, Catholics appear to be more

accepting of retardation than Protestants or Jews, and Hutterites are so accepting that they will not institutionalize any retarded member of their community (Eaton and Weil, 1955; Farber,
1960a, 1960b; Kramm, 1963; Stone and Parnicky, 1965; Zui,
1959; Zuk et al., 1967). Many well-known books and articles
written by parents of retarded children (for example, Abraham,
1958; Buck, 1950; Frank, 1952; Gant, 1957; Junker, 1964; Logan,
1962; Rogers, 1953; Stout, 1959) strongly reflect value conflicts
and both adaptive and maladaptive ways of responding. There
have been numerous reports of parents who were well equipped
with intelligence and resources who found themselves blocked by
inner value conflicts from raising or relating to their retarded
children; other families have struggled hard against poverty and
situational burdens and managed to succeed in raising retarded
children to productive citizenship.

It follows from the above that many parents have conflicts
about a retarded child not because the child is an extraordinary
burden of care, but because they intensely disvalue the meaning
(Ryckman and Henderson, 1965) which the child represents.
Thus, a value conflict is a very subjective thing but no less real
or necessarily less stressful to one family than the burdens of

care are to another. A parental value conflict may result in various degrees of emotional and physical rejection of their child. When mild, it may be manifested by ambivalence and overprotection; when severe it is inclined to eventuate in the child being discarded -- usually by means of institutionalization -- and perhaps even in his existence being completely denied. Unless a parent is exposed to existential management experiences or spontaneously undergoes existential growth experience during the course of his life, the value conflict is likely to last a lifetime.

Appropriate existential management may include psychotherapy, but other measures may be more effective as well as efficient. One of these is counseling that is not oriented toward psychodynamics and unresolved childhood fixations but toward the meaning of life and its ultimate values. Various schools of existential thought specialize in this type of counseling, for example, the school of logotherapy. Another and very underutilized measure is religious counseling. Much, of course, depends on the selection of an appropriate pastoral or religious counselor, but most religions permit multiple positive interpretations of a retarded child (for example, Eaton and Wil, 1955; Hoffman, 1965; Zuk, 1959).

Some persons, though actively involved in a religion or church, are not aware of these interpretations. However a person is likely to accept them when exposed to them in the proper context because these interpretations, although perhaps inconsistent with other values he may hold, are consistent with the large and deeply meaningful values and beliefs that are mediated by his religion.

The rationale for a third measure of assisting parents of retarded children was apparently first fully elaborated by Weingold and Hormuth (1953). They pointed out that since value conflicts are mediated by a process of socialization involving various groupings of society, a very promising management should be group-derived resocialization. While group techniques had been used earlier, Weingold and Hormuth were the first to present a truly systematic rationale for the use of group counseling with parents experiencing conflicts in attitudes. If this rationale is valid -- and it has much face validity -- congregational support should be one of the most powerful management options because it can combine group-mediated resocialization with adaptive religious interpretation. Congregational support implies that a parish, church, or church group show its acceptance -- or continued acceptance -- of a family with a retarded child in a number of ways, both large and small. This would include friendly and frequent socialization with the family, offers of baby-sitting and other assistance, active expression of interest by the past, and so on. A major manifestation of congregational support would be the operation of Sunday School classes or day-care services for retarded children with active voluntary participation on the part of church members.

There are, of course, other alternatives. The important point is for the parent's helper to truly understand the principles and processes involved in a value conflict and then to invoke management alternatives flexibly, creatively, and in ways which take account of local and specific circumstances.

The accompanying table summarizes a theoretical framework in regard to the sources of management needs. Some normative behaviors of parents in novelty shock, in value conflict, or under reality stresses are listed; some major management needs are given; and positive and negative parental adjustments are indicated. I will now proceed to present a management strategy that is based on this management framework, and that provides practical guidance in individual cases.

A Theoretical Framework for the Management of Parents of the Retarded

Three Major Sources of Parental Management Needs

Nature of Responses	Novelty Shock	Value Conflict	Reality Stress
Normative initial parental responses	Confusion Disorganization Helplessness	Dependency Anguish Anger	Profound existential pain and insult to ego Ambivalence about acceptance of facts	Stress symptoms Deterioration of health Family tension
Management needs	Immediate supportive counseling to realign expectancies Medical-diagnostic interpretations that are realistic yet focus on positive developmental expectancies Preparation of parents for planning and utilization of services Provision of societal and peer support as by referral to parent groups	Existential type of therapy or counseling (for example, pastoral counseling) Resocialization, as with group counseling, congregational support Finding a niche for the child in the parental value system Exposure of parents to models of positive conflict resolution, as in the parent movement	Correct assessment of reality based family needs Knowledge of and rapid provision of concrete services that relieve situational demands
Adaptive parental adjustments	Acceptance of reality factors Seeking or acceptance of guidance Realignment of expectations and plans	Resolution of existential parental quandary Value change Investment of value in the child Empathy for the child	Search for resources Utilization of resources Participation in the creation of needed resources and services Placement of child outside the home where appropriate
Maladaptive parental adjustments	Rejection of child Inappropriate discarding of child Precipitous institutionalization Denial of reality Surrender to irrational guilt Conflicted management of child Withdrawal Irrational affixing of blame	Rejection of child Inappropriate institutionalization Denial of child or his condition Severe and continued ambivalence Shopping for invalid diagnoses and cures Reaction formation Conflicted management of child Sense of unfulfillment Chronic sorrow Prolonged emotional disorder	Rejection of child Premature separation from child Unnecessary institutionalization Family dissolution Passive surrender to situational demands

PROGRAMMING THE MANAGEMENT PROCESS

It is proposed that those who seek to effectively aid parents of the retarded should explore a general strategy of management which appears to have high parsimony and to be consistent with decision theory by exploring and meeting family-management needs in a rank order of immediacy of the problems, by minimizing superfluous or irrelevant assessments, and by testing management options selectively so as to maximize the probability of their effectiveness. This strategy involves three stages, which will be discussed below, and each is summarized in the accompanying chart.

Stage 1

Immediately upon referral, the family helper should assess the parents' response to the diagnosis, and work toward the generation, obtaining, and utilization of services which have immediate relevance. By intimately tying a theory of parental stress dynamics to a strategy of assessment and management, I feel that we can more confidently answer the old question: Assessment For What?

During any stage of the management cycle great care should be exercised in the use of referrals to other agencies. Often,

An Approval to Exploring/Meeting the Family-Management Needs of
Parents of the Retarded

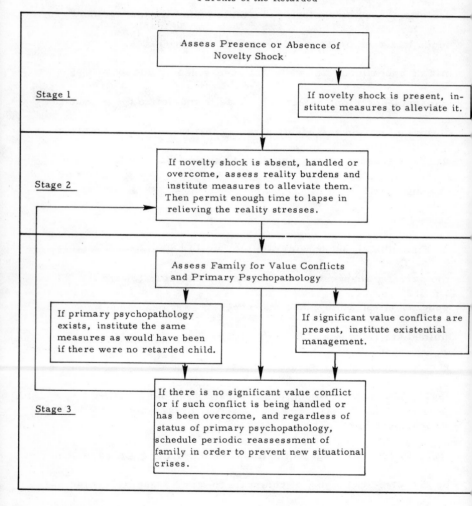

Stage 1

Assess Presence or Absence of
Novelty Shock

If novelty shock is present, institute measures to alleviate it.

Stage 2

If novelty shock is absent, handled or
overcome, assess reality burdens and
institute measures to alleviate them.
Then permit enough time to lapse in
relieving the reality stresses.

Assess Family for Value Conflicts
and Primary Psychopathology

If primary psychopathology
exists, institute the same
measures as would have been
if there were no retarded child.

If significant value conflicts are
present, institute existential
management.

Stage 3

If there is no significant value conflict
or if such conflict is being handled or
has been overcome, and regardless of
status of primary psychopathology,
schedule periodic reassessment of
family in order to prevent new situational
crises.

such referrals constitute unconscious defensive maneuvers on the part of professionals or entire agencies and may start a family on the run-about circuit. If referrals appear to be indicated, they should be accompanied by aggressive follow-through on the part of the referring professional or agency until it is ascertained that appropriate services are being provided from another source, or until a conscious and deliberate decision has been reached to terminate or suspend management. Too often, management is not terminated by a conscious decision but is permitted to "fizzle out" and casually drop out of awareness.

Stage 2

For parents in any state other than novelty shock, the realistic situational demands upon the family should be assessed. Generally, steps should then be taken to relieve these situational burdens. This may imply a number of measures such as those discussed in the section on reality stress. Until concrete relief measures have been instituted in order to alleviate the immediacy of a stressful reality it is ordinarily senseless to be concerned with problems of real or suspected psychopathology. Here it is useful to think in decision-theory terms: alleviation of reality demands might alleviate psychopathology, no matter whence its

201

source, but alleviation of psychopathology might be either impossible or of little benefit if reality demands are still excessive. Thus, concrete and direct measure that provide relatively fast relief from situational stresses not only may accomplish the greatest benefits at least cost, but also may open up the way for a more valid assessment of possible psychopathology.

Once concrete measures have been instituted, enough time should be permitted to lapse so that those stresses that can be relieved by these measures may have a chance to dissipate or at least lessen significantly. During this time, it can be expected that those signs and symptoms of family stress that can reasonably be assumed to have resulted from the situational demands will dissipate enough to permit the assessment of more deep-seated conflicts. At this point, it is time to move to the third stage of management.

Stage 3

Once it is reasonably certain that the parents are no longer in novelty shock and that the family has found some relief from the burdens of a demanding reality, the time is optimal to assess the following: "primary psychopathology," that is, problems of personal adjustment which may be aggravated by the presence of a retarded family member but which basically have their origin elsewhere; and personal and social values and attitudes relative

to retardation which interfere with adaptive behavior.

Primary psychopathology can be managed much as it would

be if the retarded family member were not retarded. Value con-

flicts would be managed as indicated in the earlier section on

value conflicts.

General Remarks about the Proposed Family Management Cycle

No matter what problems existed, what management was

conducted, or what results were obtained families should be sched-

uled for periodic reassessments. Novelty shock due to retardation

is almost always a nonrecurring event of short duration. Value

crises tend to be long-term, but once resolved they are not likely

to move from cycle to cycle and from crisis to crisis as the re-

tarded child and his family pass through various developmental

life stages. Thus, reassessment should be oriented primarily

toward situational stresses. Reassessment may take place at

regular intervals or during those developmental phases most

likely to be fraught with stress. At any rate, management of

families will increasingly be perceived, not as a one-shot effort,

but as a life-long process. We will probably see the development

of services and service delivery systems more appropriate to such

a conceptualization than exist at present.

One often hears the cliche that assessment should be a continuing process. From the above, it is obvious that assessment
of family functioning is an integral part of the management cycle.
One can thus question that meaningfulness of the present custom
of conducting the most comprehensive assessment prior to the
provision of significant amounts of services. The argument is
often advanced that it takes a thorough assessment in order to
determine the need for any type of service. I believe this view
to be erroneous. Many families are under such obvious environmental stress that needed relief measure can be identified by any
intelligent citizen who has a general familiarity with available
resources. Perhaps the initial evaluation should be more modest
in extent, attempting mostly to ascertain existence of novelty shock,
the extent to which the child's condition warrants concern about
the future, and the needs for immediate, stress-relieving services
have been initiated, after the crisis atmosphere has dissipated,
and after the parents have become more oriented toward problem-
solving by means of service utilization.

Most important, the predictive function of assessment
probably should be greatly de-emphasized. Instead, assessment
of the child should be used more to help select the optimal developmental services and to measure the apparent response to such

services. Such a reconceptualization would not only be more practical but would also help in shifting parental concern away from an unpredictable and often distorted view of the future, which is likely to create a feeling of impotence and are found in three major phenomena: novelty shock, value conflicts, and reality stresses. A practical management strategy which encompasses a cycle of assessments, decisions, and service provisions has also been presented.

CONCLUSION

The provision of services to the families of the retarded can be justified by pointing to three potential beneficiaries of such services. First there is the retarded person himself, whose life course can be profoundly affected by the services he receives. Often, the only way to help him and to insure that services rendered to him are not wasted is by working with and through the family. Second, services may provide significant or even crucial assistance to members of the family so that they (singly or as a unit) can function in a relatively normal or at least adequate fashion. Third, society itself benefits by preventing individual and family disorganization or the need for even more costly services later.

I have presented a broad concept of management, a highly selective literature review, and a theory proposing that management needs of families of the retarded parents appear to be experiencing novelty shock. If so, emotional support as well as information, education, facts, and reading matter should be provided, and the child's condition should be interpreted in a way that places a realistic emphasis on positive developmental expectations and resources likely to be available in the future. Also, joining of the parent movement should be encouraged, and the necessary names, addresses, phone numbers, brochures, and so on should be provided. Such help should be delivered as speedily as possible; a matter of days or even hours might make a difference in the future life course of the family. If the parents do not appear to be in novelty shock, stage 2 is invoked; this should also be done once parents pass from novelty shock into a period of stress caused by awareness of the realistic burdens of caring for a handicapped child.

REFERENCES

Abraham, W. Barbara: A prologue. New York: Holt, Rinehart & Company, 1958.

Aldrich, C. A. Preventive medicine and mongolism. American Journal of Mental Deficiency, 1947, 52, 127-129.

Beddie, A., & Osmond, H. Mothers, mongols and mores. Canadian Medical Association Journal, 1955, 73, 167-170.

Buck, P. The child who never grew. New York: John Day. 1950.

Eaton, J. W., & Weil, R. J. Culture and mental disorders: A comparative study of the Hutterites and other populations. Glencoe, Ill.: Free Press, 1955.

Farber, B. Effects of a severely mentally retarded child on family integration. Monographs of the Society for Research in Child Development, 1959, 24, (2).

Farber, B. Perceptions of crisis and related variables and the impact of a retarded child on the mother. Journal of Health and Human Behavior, 1960, 1, 108-118, (a).

Farber, B. Family organization in crisis: Maintenance of integration in families with a severely mentally retarded child. Monographs of the Society for Research in Child Development, 1960, 25(1), (b).

Frank, J. P. My son's story. New York: Alfred A. Knopf, Inc., 1952.

Gant, S. One of those: The progress of a mongoloid child. New York: Pageant, 1957.

Hoffman, J. L. Mental retardation, religious values, and psychiatric universals. American Journal Psychiatry, 1965, 121, 885-889.

Holt, K. S. Home care of severely retarded children. Pediatrics, 1958, 22, 744-755.

Junker, K. S. The child in the glass ball. New York: Abingdon Press, 1964.

Kramm, E. R. Families of mongoloid children. Washington: U.S. Government Printing Office, 1963.

Logan, H. My child is mentally retarded. Nursing Outlook, 1962, 10, 445-448.

Menolascino, F. J. Psychiatric aspects of mental retardation in children under eight. American Journal Orthopsychiatry, 1965, 35, 852-861.

McDonald, E. T. Understand those feelings. Pittsburgh: Stanwix House, 1962.

Olshansky, S. Chronic sorrow: A response to having a mentally defective child. Social Casework, 1962, 43, 190-193.

Olshansky, S. Parent response to a mentally defective child. Mental Retardation, 1966, 4(4), 21-23.

Rogers, D. E. Angel unaware. Westwood, N. J.: Fleming H. Revell, 1953.

Ross, A. O. The exceptional child in the family. New York: Grune & Stratton, 1964.

Rychman, D. B., & Henderson, R. A. The meaning of a retarded child for his parents: A focus for counselors. Mental Retardation, dation, 1965, 3(4), 4-7.

Solnit, A. J., & Stark, M. H. Mourning and the birth of a defective child. Psychoanalytical Study of Childhood, 1961, 16, 523-537.

Solomons, G. Counseling parents of the retarded: The interpretation interview. In F. J. Menolascino (Ed.), Psychiatric Approaches to Mental Retardation. New York: Basic Books, Inc., 1970, pp. 455-474.

Stone, N. D., & Parnicky, J. J. Factors associated with parental decisions to institutionalize mongoloid children. Training School Bulletin, 1965, 61, 163-172.

Stout, L. I reclaimed my child. Philadelphia, Pa.: Chilton, 1959.

Tizard, J., & Grad, J. C. The mentally handicapped and their families: A Social Survey. London: Oxford University Press, 1961.

Waskowitz, C. H. The parents of retarded children speak for themselves. Journal of Pediatrics, 1959, 54, 319-329.

Weingold, J. T., & Hormuth, R. P. Group guidance of parents of mentally retarded children. Journal Clinical Psychology, 1953, 9, 118-124.

Wolfensberger, W. Diagnosis diagnosed. Journal of Mental Subnormality, 1965, 11, 62-70.

Wolfensberger, W. Counseling the parents of the retarded. In A. A. Baumeister (Ed.), Mental retardation: Appraisal, education, and rehabilitation. Chicago, Ill.: Aldine Press, 1967, pp. 329-400.

Wolfensberger, W. The origin and nature of our institutional models. In R. Kugel and W. Wolfensberger (Eds.), Changing patterns in residential services for the mentally retarded. Washington: President's Committee on Mental Retardation, 1969, pp. 59-171. (a)

Wolfensberger, W. & Menolascino, F. J. Methodological Considerations in Evaluating the Intelligance-Enhancing Properties of Drugs. In F. J. Menolascino (Ed.), Psychiatric Approaches to Mental Retardation. New York: Basic Books, Inc., 1970, pp. 399-421.

Zuk, G. H. The religious factor and the role of guilt in parental acceptance of the retarded child. American Journal Mental Deficiency, 1959, 64, 139-147.

Zuk, G. H., Miller, R. L., Bartram, J. B., & Kling, F. Maternal acceptance of retarded children: A questionnaire study of attitudes and religious background. Child Development, 1961, 32, 525-540.

Zwerling, I. Initial counseling of parents with mentally retarded children. Journal Pediatrics, 1954, 44, 469-479.

THE ROLE OF PARENT ASSOCIATIONS IN OBTAINING AND MONITORING NORMALIZED SERVICES FOR THE MENTALLY RETARDED

Frank J. Menolascino

During the last twenty-four years, the National Association for Retarded Citizens (N. A. R. C.) has had the courage to initially light some candles of hope for our retarded citizens, then converted to the kerosene lamp in the mid-'fifties to help illuminate biomedical research interests and efforts, switched to an electric flooding of the entire plight of the retarded in the early 'sixties, and now in the 'seventies, it stands ready with its laser beam to bring the retarded truly out of the shadows of destructive folklore and mythology, a non-human societal status, and being the passive pawns of only temporarily interested professional groups. Today we are in an exciting time and on the threshold of providing truly normalizing programs and expectations for the mentally retarded! I recently attended an annual convention of a state association for retarded citizens which is actively pushing itself past this threshold into some of the major ideological programmatic challenges of the 'seventies. On their program were the following topics: A) Pre-school education for the retarded child at home; B) Special education drop-out; the multiply handicapped children; C) Work and recreation for the mentally retarded -- programs for independence and risk; D) Sexual guidance; E) Community homes for the retarded What should they be like and offer? F) The voice of the con-

210

sumer: The National Association for Retarded Citizens and the
mentally retarded citizens themselves; and G) Advocacy -- who
will care and take care? These challenges concerning the future
directions of ideology and programming were discussed at the
most important level of change: by the advocates of the actual
consumer of current-future services for the retarded!

In this chapter, the modern ideology and models of service
which will bring normalizing services for the mentally retarded
and the concepts and programmatic implications of the developmental model and the principle of normalization will be renewed.
The major stumbling blocks which impede the active implementation of these concepts and their implications -- professional
morality -- will then be discussed at some length. Finally, this
chapter will stress the future innovations of providing services
for the mentally retarded which I feel can and must be attained in
the 'seventies.

Contemporary Services for the Mentally Retarded

Contemporary western society places high social importance
on such attributes as intelligent behavior, social adaptability,
emotional dependence, economic self-efficiency, and physical
attractiveness. Since the mentally retarded individuals do not
meet one or more of these "expected" criteria, they are in dire

need of normalization as part of their overall developmental programming so that they are able to meet and/or approximate these
attributes and thus actively fit into the world around them. Yet,
today we notice that most of the generic programs for the mentally
retarded primarily reflect: A) the retarded as a "sick" person,
B) the retarded as the perpetual child, C) the retarded as a deviant from which society should be protected, and D) similar
derogatory assessments (Wolfensberger, 1969).

Therefore, future programs for the retarded must strongly
embody the twin principles of the developmental model and normalization -- so as to fulfill both the societal and individual expectations of the mentally retarded. These two principles will be
explored, reflecting on what the trends and programs for the
mentally retarded will encompass in the 'seventies.

I. The Developmental Model

There are three fundamental concepts of the developmental
model: 1) Life as change which means that all living beings are in
a constant state of change and that to remain static is to cease to
exist; professional consideration must be focused upon the internal
and external factors influencing the retarded individual, which is a
concentration on the modification of both developmental expectations

and social behavioral skills (Grossman, 1973). 2) Sequence of development, which means all organisms progress from a simple state of structure and function to a complex one and that this process is an orderly growth. 3) Flexibility of development, which means that in addition to the general sequence of development, each individual is subjected to varying stimuli from the environment, from cultural differences and from ongoing patterning from meaningful people, all of which combine to account for the variance in the rate and particulars of an individual's development. This last point is especially relevant in assessing the developmental potentials of children previously viewed as inherently hopeless or genetic cripples. Professionals have become more cognizant of the numerous interrelationships of the environmental and inherited factors of retardation, and with this, their endeavors on behalf of the retarded have been more successful.

Programs for the mentally retarded which are developmentally oriented will of necessity focus on selected areas for accelerating, decelerating, or modifying both the direction and rate of learning and behavioral changes. The goal of the developmental model is an increased concentration on providing the retarded individual with effective coping devices for his interpersonal and physical environments; this is in sharp contrast to the past/current approaches of self-preservation (custodialism) and its associated concept of the "happy mentally retarded." How many of the current "lost generation" of the retarded have primitive behavior because they are "untutored" rather than "autistic", "psychotic", or "odd"?

These foci and goals of the developmental model will produce programs which allow the retarded individual to increase his control over his environment, increase the complexity of his behavior, extend his repertoire of interpersonal skills, and maximize his human qualities. Further, developmental maximization of the retardate's human qualities leads to the second basic concept of contemporary programs for the retarded, normalization.

II. The Implications of Normalization

The concept of normalization embodies a philosophical position concerning the personal dignity and human rights of any individual, and a series of specialized service-program concepts. The direct application of both the philosophical position and the service-program concepts to the mentally retarded individual demands the utilization of services which are in the mainstream of society.

Normalization essentially refers to an attitude and approach to the retarded individual which stresses his having the opportunity to live a life as close to the normal as possible. The attitudinal

dimension stresses that the retarded have a right to developmental

opportunities as a fellow citizen, period! They are not vegetables,

mongolian idiots, or low level retardates, but rather, they are

fellow humans who have a variety of special problems in coping

with the world around them. The approach segment of this

definition of normalization encompasses a positive posture of

hope, challenge, and eyeball-to-eyeball honesty as to what can,

must, and will be done to help the retarded.

The National Association for Retarded Citizens (N. A. R. C.)

has already moved from illustrating what the retarded can do, by

providing early pilot programs (e. g. , Opportunity Centers) which

became the spur for initiation and extension of developmental day

training programs for the young moderately-severely retarded,

to obtaining legislative laws for trainable classes for the chrono-

logically developmentally older counterparts. Now the N. A. R. C.

is moving more actively towards monitoring the evolving service

patterns so that they do not degenerate into baby-sitting opera-

tions. The N. A. R. C. must push the professionals to re-focus

from singular pre-occupation with the partial approaches of cure

and treatment, for these approaches may be available to only a

few, and the organization must underscore future habilitation programs for all retarded citizens!

The following examples illustrate the application of both the
attitudinal and approach aspects of the normalization principle
in providing truly modern approaches to the mentally retarded:

(1) Programs and facilities for the mentally retarded should
be physically and socially integrated into the community. This
implies that service facilities must not be placed in physical
or social isolation. The large institutions for the retarded "up
on the hill" or "out in the sticks" obviously are the antithesis of
the normalization principle.

(2) No more retarded persons should be congregated in one
service facility than the surrounding neighborhood can readily
integrate into its services, resources, social life, etc. Placing
or maintaining an institution for the retarded of 1,000 patients in
a rural town of 2,000 does not permit integration of the retarded,
and further, it continues the tragic model of the historical "out of
sight -- out of mind" posture of the mental health people. Similarly, special education classes must be integrated into the
neighborhood school to which the retarded child can go with his
brothers and sisters rather than to a large central facility.

(3) Integration, and therefore normalization, can best be attained if the location of services follows population density and distribution patterns. This rather obvious dimension had been ignored in the era of institution building from 1900-1940. Similarly, it is being ignored in this decade as well.

(4) Services for the mentally retarded often need to be dispersed, not only across the communities of a state but even within a community. Intracommunity dispersal is virtually mandatory if integration is to be attained in a larger population center. The dispersal suggests that there must be multiple services and facilities rather than a single service or facility for a large population base; the clustering of these services (e.g., a developmental training center and a children's hostel in close geographical proximity to each other) will better serve neighborhoods within a community.

(5) Services and facilities for the retarded must meet at least the same standards as other comparable services or facilities for the non-retarded; this is neither more standards nor less. For example, developmental training centers must concentrate on scientifically sound methods for prescriptive teaching rather than baby-sitting. Residential facilities must have

the fire safety and sanitary standards of a Holiday Inn. Unfortunately, the mention of mental retardation to the usual program-facility planner seems to close a thinking valve and produces only the fire-sanitary standards of a hospital type of institution; these are not the standards of the mainstream of our society -- and hence are not normalizing.

(6) The personnel who work with the retarded must minimally have qualifications as those who work with comparable non-retarded groups. Although forward in its intent, this aspect has been repeatedly ignored as unlicensed physicians, semi-retired teachers, and similar borderline and/or troubled individuals who have typically not done too well in former community or institutional positions, have continued to be employed and permitted to ply their warped wares on the retarded.

(7) To bring about the maximum degree of encouraging the retarded to imitate the non-retarded as well as in the perception of the retarded by the public, the retarded must have maximal exposure to non-retarded fellow citizens in their communities. The physical isolation of some community-based ("edge of town") or residential facilities, and the self-imposed professional isolation of the staff members there are incongruent with the necessity to bring about normalization. The number of community-

based programs that somehow find the most lonely parts of the city against a mountain, on a hill at the edge of town or near the city dump, is confounding.

(8) The daily routines of programs and services for the retarded should be comparable to those of non-retarded persons of the same age. Yet how many institutionalized severely retarded are never permitted outdoors? How many of the moderately retarded leave their buildings only for the walk to the central dining room? The lack of daily normalizing routines for these retarded citizens is predicated on institutional policy, not on developmental realities. Daily routines of school attendance, recreational activity, and bedtime should be made as normal as possible. Seasonal changes including vacations should also be programmed as a portion of expected activities.

(9) Services for children and adults should be physically separated to reduce the probability that children will imitate the deviant behavior of their elders and because services to adults and children tend to be separated in the mainstream of current society. Residential services for the retarded should be specialized for specific types of problems or groups, because specialization can be better attained by age separation plus congregation

and dehumanization can be avoided. This approach is in sharp contrast to the omnibus (Procrustean Bed) nature of the treatment programs of current residential facilities for the retarded.

(10) The retarded person is entitled to be dressed and groomed as any other person his age; he must be taught a normal gait, normal movements, and normal expressive behavior patterns, and his diet should be so adjusted as to assure normal weight. The probabilities should be minimized that a citizen can identify a retarded person on sight; the sloppily dressed (e.g., out-of-date clothes, poor grooming, etc.) retarded child, the barefoot (and often naked) institutionalized young adult, the "bowl" haircuts, and the one piece "monkey suits" are testimonials to our current widespread programmatic "retardation" and lack of caring.

(11) As much as possible, the adult retarded, even if severely handicapped, should be provided the opportunity to engage in work that is culturally normal in type, quantity, and setting. Although it may occur in sheltered settings, work for adult retardates should approximate typically adult work (e.g., sheltered work-shops should resemble industry) rather than activities and/or settings that are commonly associated with children, with play, with recreation, or with leisure. This dimension demands a serious re-thinking of the far too frequently noted occupational-

recreational therapy activities which embody arts-and-crafts and fun-and-games approaches that keep the retarded occupied in the name of utilizing time, rather than focusing on meaningful work. This type of diversional therapy too often parades as recreational or vocational programming.

Normalization refers to concepts which are a cluster of ideas, methods, and attitudes toward the retarded as reflected in high standards of excellence in providing the needed human services, specialized programs which are integrated into the community, high expectations of the retarded in keeping with that expected from all of us in the mainstream of our society, and utilization of the available social-family services whenever possible to eliminate the notion of the retarded as a standout and in need of exotic or overtly unique types of service.

III. Amalgamation of the Developmental Model and the Concept of Normalization

The application of the concept of normalization to the mentally retarded requires the utilization of the developmental model for social-adaptive learning to enable the mentally retarded citizen to successfully cope with the outside world. Therefore, specific programs and techniques are needed for different challenges at differing developmental ages: the child needs developmental

stimulation so as to attain a full repertoire of social-adaptive

self-help skills; the adolescent principally needs socialization,

positive peer group identity, and pre-vocational training; and the

adult principally needs specific vocational training and associated

minimal (if any) help in how to live an autonomous life in general

society.

There are administrative implications of the amalgamation of

the developmental model and the normalization principle into

modern treatment programs for the retarded. Of vital importance

is the administrator's orientation and attitude particularly with

reference to what the retarded individual can do rather than the

too often voiced concern of what he cannot do! The administrator's

attitude is far more important than his educational "stripes", or

administrative experiences (e.g., 10 years as an administrator of

a large institution for the retarded is often a sign of a dedicated

state employee -- but little else!) . A positive administrative

orientation toward sound and open staff-parent relationships is

much more facilitating than the opposite -- parents as "loud

mouths who are never satisfied", or "They are ignorant," because

of their lack of training. The administrator must understand and

utilize modern management approaches in establishing and

operating a rather complex and interlocking system of services for the mentally retarded. This approach must encompass the management techniques and objectives (e.g., the cost-benefit ratio rationale) so that a developmental prescription for each retarded individual can be outlined to meet his specific needs, and it will be very beneficial in objectively demonstrating to the consumer what the current program has, is, and will be producing and delivering in specific human services. Lastly, the administrator must have a positive posture toward change itself -- he must be flexible so as to evolve with the rapidly changing expectations and opportunities for the mentally retarded citizens in our society. Application of the practical dimensions of the principle of normalization and the developmental model to the current-future programs for the retarded must permeate all service endeavors. In brief, the twin thrusts of the principle of normalization and the developmental model will permit the opening of a new spectrum of opportunities for retarded citizens.

IV. Implementation of Normalizing Services for the Retarded in the Seventies

The first step in implementation can be accomplished by bringing together the confluent trends in the NARC among professional groups which serve the retarded, and in general society to demand superb services for the retarded. These trends have come as of: 1) instantaneous communication of events, their inter-pretations, and possible alternatives; 2) the emerging power of consumer groups, which is based on an increased awareness of the unrealized group potential and which could bring about changes in major societal systems; 3) the rising costs of human services which are leading to an ever-increasing sophistication of adminis-trative and cost-service-benefit approaches aimed at specific assessment of outcomes; 4) a new wave of humanism (especially in the young) which is blurring the lines of what is normalcy or deviancy; and 5) a deep and almost brooding national introspection about individual and societal morality. For example, in the recent past the conscience of our country was deeply pricked by the Vietnam war, racial inequality, the despoiling of our physical habitat, etc., all within the context of a degree of openness and humility that permits this introspection to be actively pursued. I will return to the dimension of morality as a major thrust of all of these confluent trends in our society towards a re-affirmation of respect for the dignity of the retarded.

Secondly, it is time to start new models of service for the retarded. A review of service models during the last forty years

(Wolfensberger, 1969) reveals that virtually no new models have been initiated. During this period, the pattern has been to make mild variations on old models (on Regional Centers), and at best, to stumble over the better on the way to the best. In this last dimension parents have often unwittingly said that, "At least a 650 bed institution is better than what we have now! So why be against these new buildings -- they are better than what we now have!" In this current period of change and increased public awareness of the retarded, by permitting these smaller institutions to be built is merely to pour old wine into new bottles; there will be spawning of a new wave of buildings that will haunt us for many years to come. The strengths of the N. A. R. C. can be utilized as <u>change agents</u> for new programs and services for the retarded, rather than having cadres of thankful followers of endless dialogues that tend to mystify rather than clarify the models of care for retarded citizens. The change agent role of N. A. R. C. must embody both new program models and new manpower utilization patterns, for the failure to couple these, in the past, has strongly contributed to the current lean offerings of services.

The Nebraska Plan for the Retarded (Wolfensberger and Menolascino, 1971) was the direct result of the activities and spurring of the Nebraska Association for Retarded Children. It started a new model of services which totally embodies the principle of normalization and the developmental model, and it has provided new vistas for manpower development and utilization. The plan synthesized the total needs of the mentally retarded at all levels of retardation and chronological ages, into eleven types of programs-facilities which provide the services that any retarded citizen may need during his lifetime. These eleven programs-facilities are: 1) maintenance of life; 2) infant development; 3) child development; 4) prevocational; 5) habit shaping services; 6) structured-correctional services; 7) training hostels; 8) sheltered living setting; 9) minimal supervision setting; 10) crisis assistance unit, and 11) the five-day school (for rural settings). The Nebraska Plan represents a prototype of a contemporary regional service system (instead of a Regional Center) that can directly enrich the lives of all retarded citizens within their primary or extended family settings and within the home community. Since some currently unmet needs are those of severe-to-profoundly retarded children (the associated multiple handicaps), I would like to discuss the Maintenance of Life, Infant Development, and Child Development components of the above noted eleven-part total regional system of services for the retarded. (See Appendix).

These three services are already running smoothly in Nebraska and the first two services prompted the closing of a residential facility that is a shame to my state. We are personally and professionally committed to bringing these services to full fruition, for we feel that their successful operation will be the "acid test" of the Nebraska Plan for the Retarded. The reader has undoubtedly recognized that it is the very lack of these three services (especially "Maintenance of Life" and "Infant Development") that has provided a rationale for the current hopeless-helpless labeling of the severely and profoundly retarded and the "instant" solutions that are always being offered (e. g. , a new wing added to an old institution and/or a "new" Regional Center). In this matter the professional integrity and personal morality of the advocates of the retarded in Nebraska will be fully tested to its limits.

The ideology and practical implementation of the Nebraska Plan for the Retarded has, to date, eventuated in a situation wherein the state of Nebraska has more locally based services for its retarded citizens than any other state in this country. More importantly, the new system is actively monitored by the local A. R. C. units (illustrating that A. R. C. units must move their action efforts from <u>providing</u> services to <u>obtaining</u> the services from local-state-federal sources to assure their high quality). The new system has successfully passed the initial hurdles of cost-service benefit ratio considerations: the services range in cost from 84 cents a day for a young adult in a job station in industry to $22.60 a day for a full children's program including a specialized hostel for severely retarded older children with associated motor and/or special sensory handicaps. Simultaneously, the ubiquitous political problems, such as public officials who had viewed the new locally based services as a threat to the active nurturing of their "local public works" (e.g., state residential facilities for the retarded, re-directed state hospitals, etc.) have also been resolved by the sheer logic of programs which <u>actually work</u> to help the retarded in a direct fashion! Most importantly, the Nebraska Plan has become directly relevant to providing specialized and dispersed services of excellence to retarded citizens across Nebraska.

In the recent past, many of the prime movers of the Nebraska Plan were considered as "dreamers when it comes to money -- why it will cost over $10,000/year per client!", and we were pushed to come up with specific cost-service benefit figures on our entire range of services. Rather than harm the new services, this request for "hard" economic guidelines and expenditures proved to be powerful documentation for the objective accountability of the services provided. Yet, the institutions' personnel do not have these figures and continue to demand more money while hiding larger costs (e. g. , within separate state budgetary guidelines for renovation and construction), blatantly amalgamate disparate costs such as the Maintenance of Life service (e. g. , the "client-employee") within the same leveling magic figure called the "per diem rate" for all residents, etc. As one of our state legislators noted, "It doesn't take a superintendent to come before us to always ask for more and more money, since his secretary could do that easily! He has to be accountable for how much, where and why -- and the answers are always weak there." There are few (if any) indications that this traditional institutional posture of "Give us more money, and don't bother us with accountability" has changed or will change soon.

Thirdly, the questions and arguments that flow on and on across our country about what are the "best" service approaches for the retarded are a researchable set of questions! Indeed, the N. A. R. C. recently (1970) made a major policy decision relevant to this topic: N. A. R. C. will redirect its research thrust from biomedical research (with its prime focus on primary prevention) to operational-programmatic research (with its prime focus on enriching the lives of our current retarded citizens via secondary and tertiary prevention approaches). A brief overview of this major re-direction of N. A. R. C. 's research efforts may underscore the deep concern of this national organization of consumer's representatives to be relevant to current and future trends. The early efforts were, literally, underpinnings of the current series of Mental Retardation Research Centers across our country. For example, the overview of research findings and challenges in mental retardation that was commissioned by N. A. R. C. in the mid-'fifties and resulted in Mental Subnormality (Masland, Sarason, and Gladiorn, 1958) has been energetically followed through by N. A. R. C. via ongoing efforts on the part of truly magnificent members (such as Dr. Elizabeth Boggs) of its Governmental Affairs Committee. Today, there are twelve Mental Retardation Research Centers that have been funded under P. L. 88-164, starting in 1964. The Congress has appropriated $26, 000, 000 of federal funds, and the states and private sources supplied another $14, 000, 000 for construction of these Centers. The twelve research centers are each located in a university setting, and their focus has been on the prevention of retardation in the unborn and/or new bio-medical treatments for the very young retarded child (i. e. , mostly primary prevention and some secondary prevention).

It should be noted that the overwhelming majority of these Centers are not mission oriented. They tend to focus on providing research personnel the freedom to inquire, and focus on technical excellence (highly prized in university settings), rather than applied or nationally coordinated research efforts -- the latter being hallmarks of mission oriented research efforts. However, it appears that we currently need a more equitable balance between free inquiry and mission oriented research endeavors in mental retardation; otherwise the gap between the transmission of basic research into applied endeavors will continue its 10-15 year lag period -- to the detriment of the living retarded citizens in need of services.

The need for a balance between basic applied research and financial considerations are not the prime rationale for the recent N. A. R. C. research re-direction from bio-medical to operational-programmatic approaches for the retarded. Thus N. A. R. C. members can become initiators and/or evaluators therein! In contrast to bio-medical research endeavors wherein an M. D. or Ph. D.

degree "union card" seems to be needed to be considered qualified to discuss these matters--one notes that virtually all N. A. R. C. members have had experiences concerning operational and programmatic dimensions of service systems for the retarded. I am stressing this point because I winced repeatedly while reading a recent survey in which N. A. R. C. members disclaimed any competence to assess our past bio-medical research activities, and uniformly requested that these matters be left up to the "experts". In contrast, I vividly remember a wheat farmer from Montana reviewing for me the variety of options he felt were available for a work-study program for the retarded -- displaying in-depth operational-programmatic knowledge (replete with cost-service data!) about a topic very dear to his son and him. Or the attorney from New England who successfully completed a federal grant for a four part residential model(s) study that would throw light on current residential needs for the retarded in his area. His study, which presented testable hypotheses with great clarity, would put many Masters-Doctoral theses I have reviewed to shame! Accordingly, this new re-direction is directly in the area of expertise of N. A. R. C. members -- so they can evaluate (and utilize) the research efforts they support!

What comprises "operational-programmatic research" and what guidelines can be utilized for this N. A. R. C. research re-direction? In brief, N. A. R. C. has research to applied social-educational, behavioral, and service systems studies -- research that is directly relevant to the lives of the retarded, such as family support systems as to needed services, different programs and designs for residential settings (e. g. , which ones are best for what retardates in differing geographical and social settings, at what ages, etc.). Similarly, sociological analyses of the planning process in the community: What are the basic assumptions in community programs? What planning processes fail or succeed -- where and why? etc. Other examples of possible operational-programmatic research include areas such as the following:

(1) Ten years ago community-based hostels for the retarded were considered high risk projects. If N. A. R. C. had funded 5-10 hostels at that time in different geographic areas for different age groups, levels or types of mental retardation -- it would have learned much and pushed others to follow. Similarly, today the concept of the "Crisis Assistance Unit" is an example of a "high risk" operational research challenge. We kick this residential component around, though we really don't know how well it will work. For example, will it really relieve individual family

crises? What about program components such as costs involved and utilization rates? Can or should we mix children and adults of both sexes therein? Should such a unit be in town -- or in a vacation-type setting at the edge of town? (e.g., ease of transportation versus more recreational resources). How should we architecturally design this Crisis Assistance Unit?, etc., etc.

(2) The history of the Holtner Valve for the clinical management of hydrocephaly suggests that past similar "high risk" biomedical types of operational-programmatic research opportunities were and continue to be present. Mr. Holtner (an engineer who had a child with rapidly developing hydrocephaly) could have reached out to N.A.R.C. and said, "I have two months to try and finalize this valve for my child -- I need $2,000.00 to have a machinist turn my idea into reality." Or, N.A.R.C. could have aided him in establishing his eventual business to sell these valves by extending him a low interest loan.

(3) We need to translate currently available operational research into concrete published guidelines (e.g., like the earlier N.A.R.C. manual on how to organize a local N.A.R.C.). We now need similar manuals such as, "How to Plan a Community-Based Program of Residential Services" (or a regional network of services).

(4) Similarly, operational research endeavors could harness what we already know about applicable techniques to help the retarded. A case in point would be a review of current deficit theory research on the learning process and its translation into concrete guidelines for teaching the retarded. The questions here are: What is mental retardation -- is it a global learning disability? Or are there specific deficits in: attention, arousal, motivation, inhibition, the organization of memory (long versus short-term)? etc., etc. The deficit theory has spawned thousands of research proposals and reports. In turn, they have yielded many practical recommendations for teaching the retarded, such as operant learning and transfer of learning principles. Yet, if you ask the usual special education teacher how they could maximize their teaching approaches to the retarded, they rarely know anything about these practical recommendations! Why? Because this body of information has not been pulled together as to its practical applications for teachers at the "front lines", in contrast to the yearly (unreadable) reviews for fellow scientists. Lest I pick on teachers -- our residents in psychiatry are just recently becoming acquainted with operant learning-management

techniques in their teaching curriculum -- though Dr. Ogden
Lindsey illustrated the application of operant learning to disordered and/or retarded behaviors almost fifteen years ago!
An operational research project such as this one could be completed and help retarded individuals rather quickly (e.g., one to
two years).

(5) We need comprehensive cost-benefit analysis of the
relative merits of community versus institutional programming.
We could help put to rest the ongoing arguments (on both sides!)
as to the relative service-cost relationships between different
institutional settings and community systems of service (Balla,
Butterfield and Ligler, 1974). For example, there is rapidly
developing in our country a "Scandinavian backlash" phenomena
concerning whether affluent America can "really afford" the
approaches of the "socialists" in Scandinavia. This is a researchable set of issues that have direct reference to our local-state-
national approaches and attitudes toward the retarded. Such a
study should lean heavily upon the expertise available among
many of our economist colleagues. (Conley, 1973). I have mentioned our current Nebraska experiences on the cost-service
benefit ratio and its relationship to accountability -- this we

should study further to assess its strengths and weaknesses in differing socio-economic populations and geographical settings.

(6) A study of representative systems for coordinating community services for the retarded -- on the basis of which a model for an effectively coordinated system of services could be developed. This issue stems from my experience that, in many instances, agencies purportedly established for the purpose of service coordination (e.g., regional mental health and mental retardation centers) primarily provide overly elaborate diagnostic procedures and tend to shunt parents from one inappropriate service possibility to another. It is my personal feeling that such ineffective coordination has done much to unfairly contribute to the stereotype of the parent of the retarded as a diagnosis and/or service shopper.

(7) A study of Citizen Advocacy programs, developed on the basis of the model provided by Dr. W. Wolfensberger, would be aimed at determining their effectiveness in insuring the legal and personal rights of, and provisions of meaningful services to, our mentally retarded citizens. (Wolfensberger and Zauha 1973).

(8) A demonstration and investigation of a total developmental prosthetic environment -- especially for the severe-to-profoundly retarded non-ambulatory person. Though much has been written

about this applied research challenge, few examples of this service are present in our country today. Not only would this type of programmatic research directly aid the profoundly retarded citizen -- it can be an excellent example of what we can do for these citizens and spur societal changes as to the current attitudes of hopelessness in this specific area of programmatic endeavor.

(9) Lastly, we can try to focus on what operational-programmatic trends are now on the horizon. In other words, we would dedicate ourselves to selectively support, with seed money, the glimpses of the future in the current researcher's eyes -- and help them complete pilot programs before they get ready to go to state-federal sources for "big money" requests for larger scale operational-programmatic research endeavors. An example here could be the establishment of rigidly designed psycho-pharmacological studies to assess the effectiveness of some of the recently described purported memory and learning enhancers.

These general and specific types of operational-programmatic research efforts can have an immediate impact on the retardate's current-future life. This new re-direction of N. A. R. C's research efforts will give it the results needed to answer both our current unquestioned answers to unanswered questions and stop our stumbling over the better on the way to the best services for our retarded citizens.

V.   Professional Morality

> "Am I mad that I should cherish that which
> Bears but bitter fruit?
> I will tear it from my bosom, though my
> Heart be at its root."

Lord Tennyson

I have left to the end, though I have touched on it briefly, earlier, a dimension of our current parental-professional efforts, which focuses on the issue of morality. I approach this dimension with some trepidation because morality is so often in the eye and soul of the beholder, and it is a topic which has a high propensity for making more "enemies" for a fellow like me!   Yet, events of the past few months have made me even more convinced that the morality of a man is measured by what he stands for and does, rather than the social graces that seem to lead to ever increasing numbers of "friends" who don't seem to disagree about anything! A year ago, some of my colleagues had begun to convince me that the slow, steady approach to changing the tragic plight of our institutionalized retarded citizens was the "cool way" to get the job done, and the "keep plugging away in a gentle fashion from inside of the system" approach would change these large congregate mausoleums for the living dead. In other words, be tactful, and as surely as the day follows night, my fellow professionals across this country would surely see the "Ford Light" of the new approaches to the retarded, and do what is right; after all, they are professionals! Even my wife said I was becoming more polite to those personal contacts who still mouth sweet emptinesses about "those retarded folks who are hopeless and belong out in the country with their own kind so that they can't bother anyone."

Recently I attended a national meeting of an organization of professionals whose major vocational endeavor is in providing services for the retarded. Historically, this organization stems from the early meetings of superintendents of institutions for the retarded, and remains entrenched with these "old and not-so-old guard" professional personnel. I had been invited to present a paper on a panel concerning behavioral problems in the retarded. Since this dimension of the retarded is my favorite vocation-avocation, I readily agreed to attend and present a paper. I was the second presenter, and the first presenter was an

experienced psychologist who presented a paper which was inno-
cently listed in the program as, "Psychological Issues in Institutionalization of the Mentally Retarded." He prefaced his
presentation by remarking that he had just changed jobs -- from
an institution in the midwest, to a university setting in another
region of our country. He stated that in the interval between the
time he had agreed to present the paper and the day of the
presentation he had, A) deeply searched his reasons for being
at this institution for the last six years, and his possible service
value to the retarded citizens therein; B) wondered why the
community programs (which he had both visited and studied)
were not more actively accepted by his institutional colleagues,
C) re-written his paper, and D) decided to leave his institutional
position.

It was a gut-level paper that succinctly questioned both the
validity and morality of professionals who man institutional
settings for the retarded which have lost their ideological underpinnings and were of minimal value to the retarded citizens
therein -- preparing them for a life of personal oblivion in a
wasteland of humanity. He strongly recommended that institutions for the retarded be rapidly phased out while simultaneously

a wide array of community-based programs were actively started, embellished, and brought to fruition. It was an excellent paper which was presented with gusto! Mindful of the admonitions of my colleagues and wife to "play it cool", I inwardly decided not to partake in the rather heated discussion that followed. The audience, which is typical of this organization (mostly institution- al-based professionals), threw their old rocks at the paper presenter: "Parents like the institutions, they don't want their retarded kids"; "Community-based programs don't and can't work!"; "We haven't failed the communities, they have failed us -- no money!"; "We have outstanding programs, it's just that no one appreciated them, and we don't brag about them..."; etc., etc. The presenter handled these "hack" statements -- which have lulled generations of institutionalized retarded citizens (and the professionals who serve as their gatekeepers) into oblivion-- with ease. Expectedly, his detractors in the audience became louder and more abusive. Then, like a bolt out the blue, a fellow in the second row got to his feet, pointed at me, and said, "And you, Menolascino, you are one of those trouble makers that go around this country spreading lies about what can be done for the retarded. You lie to parents, and you use phony numbers and fancy cliches when you talk to legislators. Community programs cannot work. I know because the retarded have to be put away for their own sake and for the sanity of their parents. So don't just sit there, say something!" Well, I did, for this man had recently been removed as a superintendent of an institution like those depicted in Christmas in Purgatory (Blatt and Kaplan, 1966). Yet he had not learned, in the twilight of his professional career, that the parents of the retarded in that state have seen through this aimless and cruel warehousing of the retarded. Rather than talk about "lies"--since there are none, past or present -- I focused on the morality of any professional who does not actively utilize the knowledge which we do have to aid the retarded, and who, instead, continues his own personal mythology and its associated dehumanization of the retarded. In brief, I rather savagely told this man to step aside, and let the new wave of hope for the retarded re-vitalize our collective faith and trust that current ideologies (e. g. , normalization and the developmental model) can bring new horizons of personal dignity to our fellow retarded citizens!

Yet the day had just begun and that afternoon there was a symposium on architectural challenges in providing residential settings for the retarded. One of the speakers began by discussing normalization, the "non-medical model", specialization of services, etc. It sounded like a true escape from the old guard pow-wow of that morning. Then a document which pertained to the speaker's topic was distributed to the audience. The document was a plan for a four hundred bed institution out in the countryside in a large state. Like some cruel parody, the document effused modern concepts as a slick preamble to cover the dungheap of an institutional scheme! Excerpts were included, such as, "It was the belief of the mental health experts in _____ that residents of state facilities for the mentally retarded have often been relegated to second-class citizenship, have been subjected to a dehumanizing process, and have been denied their basic human and civil rights. Too often state facilities have been "make believe" hospitals in their structuring, staffing, and control, when in fact a large percentage of patients do not require medical care. The important needs of the mentally retarded, i.e., aid in language, social, emotional and basic behavioral development has been severely neglected. The philosophy of _____ Government is predicated on the belief that the mentally retarded, as individuals and members of society, are

244

entitled to the same rights and privileges due all citizens. It follows then that the state program for new residential centers should be based on the concept of "normalization" ... that the mentally retarded should have available to them the patterns and conditions of everyday life which are as close as possible to the norms and patterns of mainstream society."

Following this preface, there were a number of line drawings that depicted the retarded in a variety of "homelike settings." The drawings were embellished with accompanying vignettes such as, "Come with me to touch, to taste, to feel the world: for this is what is real"; "Clustered homes amid the green of grass and trees. Walk with me. Enjoy the gentle breeze"; "Drink in the warm, the love, the sound you hear; where life is full of hope without fear." etc. Are these the realities of life which you and I -- presumably the "normals" -- experience in the normalizing mainstreams of our communities? More disturbing, and in my opinion grossly misleading, was an architectural rendering and its accompanying title narratives which commenced with the heading, "A Planned Community": "Clusters of single-story condominiums set among green belts, playgrounds, winding walkways, overlooking a crystal lagoon..."; "A complete community environment where the mentally retarded can experience the same rights and privileges as due all citizens ... where the exceptional are not an exception." One must ask: are these the standards of mainstream society? Who has the everyday luxury of a "crystal lagoon"? Doesn't a "complete community" sound like the sour old wine of current institutions for the retarded in a new bottle? The phrase, "...where the exceptional are not an exception", sounds like a modern day rationalization to float a "colony for the deviants", whether they be "exceptional" via tuberculosis, leprosy, epilepsy, mental retardation, etc., etc.

Rather than focus more on this tragic proof of Santayana's admonition that "...he who does not know the past is committed to repeat its errors", we must ask: "Have we, the purported advocates of the retarded learned so little these last fifty years? Are we really that "retarded"? "Or has our courage toward challenging the professional morality of such schemes become of such low voltage that we accept these modern day "solutions" which permit planners to gratify their "edifice complexes"? In my opinion, the price for us will be restless sleep and increasingly gnawing consciences for permitting the clarion call of St. Matthew --"Inasmuch as ye have done it unto one of the least of these My brethren, ye have done it unto Me" -- to be muted. <u>True</u>, a 400 bed facility is "better" than two of the current institutions for the retarded in this particular state which are among the largest institutions for the retarded in the world. <u>True</u>, this state is affluent and probably can afford the $35 a day per client projected cost at this "new" facility -- we cannot (luckily) in Nebraska. True, the statement, "They will receive up to four hours of programming a day" -- is far better than <u>most</u> current institutional programming schedules for the retarded. However, must we stumble over the "better" on our way to seeking and demanding the best for our retarded children and adults? The entire presentation and accompanying brochure bring clear validation to Samuel Gridley Howe's observation over 120 years ago: "As it is with individuals, so it is with communities: and society moved by pity for some special form of suffering, hastens to build up establishments which sometimes increase the very evil which it wishes to lessen."

This type of presentation, which is aimed at mystifying rather than clarifying, should upset all professionals who purport to be knowledgeable about current programmatic needs for the retarded. It should move us to speak out against these "new" replicas of the tragic models of the past. Why? Because our morality demands that we directly challenge these "modern" planners who want to keep our retarded citizens out in the wasteland. It is they who, out of disrespect for the dignity of the retarded, send them out to the "new colony for the deviants". It is they who cause our children with, for example, Down's Syndrome (which is glibly referred to in this pamphlet as an example of severe retardation) to live out the professional's distorted value judgement of their minimal developmental expectancy (Menolascino, 1974) to be viewed as ideal candidates for a tragic and often lifelong trip away from their loved ones-- replete with minimal programming and growth opportunities.

Yet we do have viable alternatives for these children in their home communities! Lest the reader feels that I am sidestepping the "real" issue of the severe-profoundly retarded (since the individuals with Down's Syndrome are not frequent inhabitors of this range of intellectual distribution) the previously noted "Maintenance of Life" and "Infant Development" components of the Nebraska Plan for the Retarded are community-based services. Indeed, it is my opinion that factors which have not permitted a more active implementation--on a national scale--

of community-based alternatives for severe-profoundly retarded individuals are professional myopia and laziness, and the prevalent negative professional morality-value judgments concerning these citizens.

Normalization of the retarded takes place in our homes and in our communities -- these are the mainstreams of our society. We must question the morality of those who prostitute modern concepts to crucify the retarded in their old or modern colonies for the deviants. As advocates of the retarded, it is, in my opinion, our moral obligation that we directly confront those people -- at any level of our society -- who say one thing and then do just the opposite. Rather than fear reprisal, wanting to avoid being termed "troublemakers" or "loud mouths", I feel that we are fulfilling our true role as advocates of the retarded. Indeed, as the advocates of the past-current-future consumers of these residential services -- we owe it to those in planning-policy positions to call to a halt these continuing fruitless efforts, and point out alternative models of service that will deliver the needed services in a manner which permits objective evaluation and accountability.

The sins of one generation have continued to haunt us in the areas of residential services for the retarded. Yet, if we do not utilize the knowledge we now have to seek and start new alter-

natives to these ongoing schizophrenic solutions to the needs of

our retarded citizens -- we shall all live to share our mutual

guilt.

Community-based programs cannot possibly be the miser-

able failures that our human warehouses for the retarded have

been these last almost 50 years! The evolving community-based

programs need us on a people-to-people basis within the "glass

bowl of the community" -- where all can see our efforts -- since

there is nothing to hide, no humanity to deny, and above all:

there is a great joy in creating a system that we will all be proud

to offer to those whose pathways in this world are uneven or

stormy. We can then sleep soundly -- between our days of

monitoring the new that we have both created and can view with-

out haunted consciences. To do less, such as in the numerous

projected not-so-small institutions called Regional Centers

which are being considered across our country is, in my opinion,

to default and agree that N. A. R. C. is powerless, that the candles

of hope have burned down, that the developmental stimulation and

normalization we have enjoyed is not "good" for the retarded,

and that our retarded citizens are less human and less deserving of provisions for self-fulfillment than you or me! To me, these negative constructs hinge around a personal and professional moral crisis of values -- a challenge which N. A. R. C. has met these last twenty-four years with direct action (and results!). Similarly, we must bring to full fruition the principles and practices embodied in the concepts of normalization and the developmental model to our fellow retarded citizens in the 'seventies. In this manner we can bring equal justice to the mentally retarded!

SUMMARY

We stand today just over the threshold of the 'seventies in our continuing commitment to provide developmentally oriented services within normalizing settings for our mentally retarded citizens. The principle of normalization for the retarded can only be denied if we feel that they are less than us -- or non-human. Similarly, the developmental model is applicable to even single celled amoeba -- why not to the ever more complex (and interesting!) fellow citizen who just happens to be retarded? The confluence of societal trends towards a new humanism that stresses the inalienable rights of all God's children, coupled

with the change agent posture of N. A. R. C. towards the future --
can capture these two ideologies of human management, and
start, then, new models of superb community-based services
for the retarded. Concomitantly, we can honestly research
the unquestioned answers to unanswered questions via the
newly redirected efforts of the N. A. R. C. research thrust. This
is the type of posture and commitment which will, in my opinion,
permit us to go from our past and current scattering of candles
of hope to the utilization of modern "laser beam" technology that
will cut through the cloud of "helpless and hopeless", and permit
us to enrich the lives of retarded citizens across our country.

APPENDIX

Three Components of a Locally-Based Service for the Severely
Retarded

Residential Service Type 1 (Maintenance of Life)

Some retarded individuals are so impaired as to require
primarily those services necessary to sustain life. The profession most suited to offer this service is the medical profession
and its related disciplines. Therefore, a residential service is

needed that has a strong medical emphasis, that is administered by medical personnel, and that operates on the hospital model. Facilities to provide such service should be placed in close proximity to medical centers. Such a complex should be sub-divided into a number of units, according to age and to some degree by sex. Care should be taken that individuals will be placed in this facility not merely because they are multiply handicapped, but because they do, in fact, require medical care more than any other single service.

While need for most residential services will decline as non-residential services increase, the need for type 1 services is not likely to decline substantially, as such a service is not readily rendered in a quality medical context, and present mortality rates of this group can be expected to decline considerably.

Residential Service Type 2 (Infant Nursery)

Type 2 services are for presumably retarded infants and children up to the chronological ages of 3-5 who do not require maintenance-of-life type of care. Some conditions frequently associated with mental retardation, such as mongolism, can be diagnosed in newborn infants. Often, such children are likely to be multiply handicapped, but the extent of future handicap and retardation can usually not be predicted with absolute confidence, and most such children can be adequately managed in the home if parents receive counseling and assistance. However, some such children are rejected, or are left homeless because of family disintegration, illegitimacy, etc. Unless foster homes can be found, or unless families or relatives can, with counseling, be persuaded to keep them -- such children will require residential care. It is for these children that an infant nursery service is necessary.

The orientation of this service is toward nurturant development of infants and young children until basic self-help functions such as walking, feeding, some communication, and some toilet training has been accomplished. Accordingly, developmentally oriented nurses and child development personnel are the major staff personnel required. Eventually, these children must be transferred to other services such as Child Development and related residential components. A few of the beds of this service might, upon occasion, be used for crisis assistance function so as to accept retarded children whose families undergo severe stresses (e.g., illness, death, parents have to travel, etc.).

In planning for the number of beds required, it should be kept in mind that for some of these children, the need for residential care may be temporary since (a) some families will reconstitute themselves; (b) some will accept the infant after initial rejection if they receive some counseling; and (c) foster care is increasingly found feasible with this group.

Residential Service Type 3 (Child Development)

This service is for children who are no longer infants and who do not require maintenance-of-life services. The anticipated age range here needs numerous units of 6-10 children each, with some degree of specialization. We have found it prudent to think in terms of four subtypes; older chronological age-higher functioning, and younger chronological age-lower functioning children. No division by sex appears to be necessary in this service.

Emphasis in this type of service is on child development. On the younger and/or lower levels, there is emphasis on completing mastery of self-help and social skills, to the degree that the children do not already have these skills upon entry into the program. Thus, the children are taught toileting, feeding, dressing, speech, social courtesies, etc. On the higher and/or older levels, many of the children are sent to local public school classes for the moderate or severely retarded. Special developmental programs have been established for those children who are not accepted by the public schools. Such programs are not operated in the living facilities, but at Developmental Day Care Centers which are adjacent to type 3 Residential Services.

The type 3 residential service is administered by a child development specialist, and various of the component units are headed either by child specialists or special educators. Some of the units in this residential type are operated by psychologists employing operant behavior shaping approach. However, this type of residence tenders itself very well to the use of living-in houseparents who assume long-term and intensive parent-like functions under the administration of professionals. College students -- who usually live in and can work odd hours -- have been found to be most effective as houseparent assistants in these Child Developmental Residential settings.

REFERENCES

Balla, D. A., Butterfield, E. C., & Zigler, E. Effects of
institutionalization on retarded children: A longitudinal
cross institutional investigation. American Journal of
Mental Deficiency, 1974, 78(5), 530-549.

Blatt, B., & Kaplan, F. Christmas in purgatory. Boston:
Allyn & Bacon, 1966.

Conley, R. W. The economics of mental retardation. Baltimore:
Johns Hopkins University Press, 1973.

Masland, R. L., & Sarason, S. B., & Gladwin, R. Mental
subnormality: Biological psychological and cultural factors.
New York. Basic Books, 1958.

Menolascino, F. J. Developmental Attainments in Down's
syndrome. Mental Retardation, 1974. (in press).

Mental Retardation News 1971.

Wolfensberger, W. The origin and nature of our institutional
models. In Kugel, R. B. & Wolfensberger, W. (Eds.),
Changing patterns in residential services for the retarded.
Washington, D. C. Government Printing Office, 1969, pp.
59-172.

Wolfensberger, W. & Menolascino. F. J. Reflections on recent
mental retardation developments in Nebraska. Mental
Retardation, 1970, 8(6), 20-27.

Wolfensberger, W. & Zauha, H. Citizen advocacy. Toronto.
National Institute of Mental Retardation, 1973.

A NORMAL LIFE
Robert Coleman

In the first six years of his life, Darren never had much more of an identity than the name on his medical records. Institutionalized and signed over to the state by his now forgotten mother, Darren adapted to the timeless institutional cocoon by withdrawing into himself. He never learned to walk nor to talk. His motor skills and social learning extended not far beyond a quick reach at the dinner table and an alert and fearful eye for strange persons and situations.

Two years later, Darren's world is no longer an institutional gray. Darren has a dog and a cat, toys, and a room of his own; but most of all, he has parents, Rose and Erland Andersen of Omaha. Their love of Darren and dedication to his growth have, in a real sense, created a person and a personality out of the silent, staring child they brought home from the institution. The Andersens, who are ENCOR developmental parents, recently became Darren's permanent legal guardians.

Darren's past is largely a mystery to the Andersens. They can only imagine the unremitting bleakness of Darren's early years that, they feel, badly stunted his physical and mental potential. They gain clues of his early experiences from his sometimes startled reactions, though after two years they seldom see these behaviors. Darren's first reaction to a flower, Rose recalls, was a frightened shriek; grass was equally a source of terror to him. But no tears. Even today, disappointment or perhaps a scolding are the only occasions that bring tears to Darren's eyes.

Happily, most of Darren's fears have evaporated since he learned to walk, an achievement that contradicted the predictions of specialists. His greater physical independence and emotional security now permit him to build his skills and interests at the dictates of his by now well-developed curiosity. In addition to dressing and learning

self-care skills, Darren shows a surprising ability to amuse himself
independently with his toys and record player and the large number of
songs he has learned to sing. For his parents, these are the rewards
for their patience and the diligence with which they have tried to teach
Darren to develop his awareness and abilities. Rather than resent
the cruel and uncaring past that added to Darren's possibly inherent
limitations, Rose and Erland are inclined to let the past die, as it
has for Darren. Rather, they are content to live in Darren's present,
delighting in the small gestures and actions that daily mark a growth
in his skills in living and learning.

Darren's learning to walk did not come easily, either for him or for Erland. With exercises, and then with daily tours around the block, Erland forced a loudly protesting Darren first to walk falteringly, and then to walk alone. Today, Darren looks forward to his daily hike with his father, particularly when they head for the hamburger stand. Darren walks without aid, and usually shakes off any assistance; Erland walks behind, offering Darren help only if necessary.

At ENCOR's West Developmental Center, Darren is an earnest student, good-natured and hard working. Darren is expected to attend a public school in September, 1974; thus his teachers work hard on the motor and language skills in which Darren will face a new challenge.

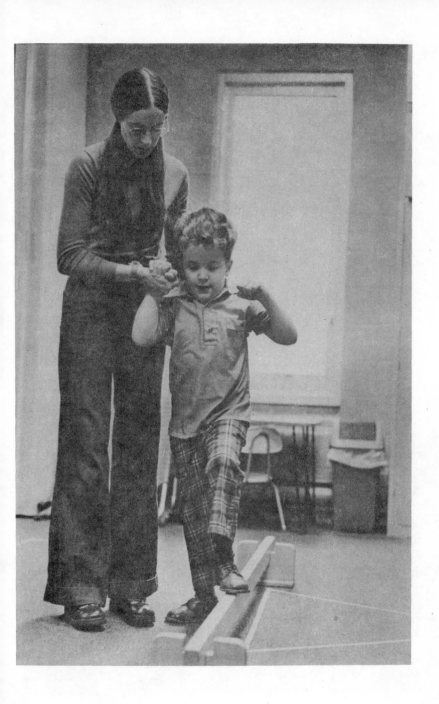

As a result of their frequent walks through the neighborhood, Darren and Erland are well-known to boys and girls in the area, who coax Darren out of his initial fear of riding his bike.

"Darren's first perceptions of people," says his father, "was to see them as a mass. Only lately has he come to see certain people, other than Rosie and me, as individuals." Recently, Darren gained his first "special" friend, the son of the pastor of their church. A further sign of Darren's emotional growth is the possessiveness he displays toward his father, whom he "protects" from any other children who might try to gain Erland's affection.

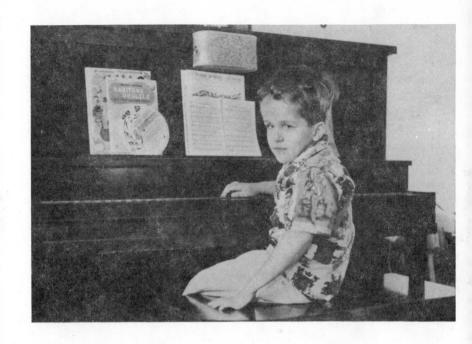

Darren's favorite "toy", initially an object of fear, is the piano. Because of his delight in music, Rose, who plays both the piano and ukelele, plans to arrange for Darren to study piano, both for the enjoyment and for the skills it would give him. The problem, she feels, is to find a teacher who would understand Darren's limits and his feelings.

At eight, Darren has, in a sense, been born again. The dim memories of a stagnant past recede, and to take their place are the achievements and striving that are now a part of him. Darren has a home and a family now, and, most of all, a future, the hope of a normal life.

CONCLUDING REMARKS
Karl Grunewald and *Una Haynes*

Near the close of the Conference the first two speakers,

Mrs. Una Haynes and Dr. Karl Grunewald, provided the following

concluding remarks as both a review of this conference and as

further elaboration of national-international trends. (Editors)

Dr. Grunewald

I really appreciate being here at this conference as I have

learned much! I think that the approach which Mrs. Haynes dis-

cussed in regard to the activities of the Cerebral Palsy Associa-

tions is also becoming more and more common in Europe --

especially in England. In America, the Society for the Cerebral

Palsied is not for the profoundly retarded, as is the National

Association for the Mentally Retarded. However, when I have

been studying in Europe, I have seen that they have special homes

for combinations of cerebral palsy and mental retardation and they

do some research. Perhaps you even know about their Journal,

which is outstanding. It is a fact that we have underestimated the

need of motor training for our mentally retarded. Yes, we have

tended to under-estimate other needs besides just toilet training!

The Cerebral Palsy Association has considered the total child psychology attitude and total environmental stimulation. It is obvious that things are now starting to come together and that we have much to learn from those working with the cerebral palsied. I am glad to see that it is beginning to happen here and in other states in the USA.

One item which I missed discussing here today as to new trends, is the help to parents to keep their profoundly retarded child in their own homes. I believe that this trend will change the whole picture in the future. For example, in Sweden, we have focused on home training techniques, and after five years we find that we are admitting fewer and fewer of the severe and profoundly mentally retarded children to our residential homes. We have many small residential homes which were specially designed for these individuals. As a matter of fact, we had overestimated the need for beds in these homes. Now these beds are used for short-term care, relief care and diagnostic evaluation, but the fact is that the need of institutional care will decline automatically, _if_ we support our parents better than we have in the past. The first support that they need is psychological support. Those who can do the most in this area are we who act as physicians when we break the news to the parents that they have a handicapped child.

There is much written on this topic now. There is a rule in Sweden that two or more pediatricians must be present when the parents are told that they have a handicapped or mentally retarded child. There is also a social worker present who knows about the various possibilities that the parents have opened to them in dealing with this problem. It is not only a medical question, it is a correction of the whole attitude from the first moment that the parents are told. With proper information, they can choose the right course. They can decide to do things their own way according to the physician's suggestions, but the one thing they know is that they are supported and that society is supportive of their problem, that special facilities are available to them -- and that they are not alone.

We tell our parents that the first alternative is <u>not</u> the institution. The first alternative is their own home. It is their child and it will always be their child. They will always have the feelings; you can never neglect that. We will help them with their emotions and we can help them with relief care of all different types, but, start in their own home. In Sweden, we pay our parents if they keep their child at home. They are paid about $1,200 a year, irrespective of their incomes. They are paid as long as they have handicapped children in their homes, up to 60 years of age and then the system changes. Our law is written so that the parents of mentally retarded children have the right to societal care. Our service organization goes out to the family and supports their needs -- from material things such as special toys and special beds, to personal support (i. e. , the mother is relieved one or two times regularly each week so that she can go out on her own knowing that there is a person in her home who is skilled enough to take over her job with her family). Families have a right to this kind of help. They have the right of having direct help in their homes. Professionals go to the home to provide the parents programs for their children -- if the parents cannot come with their child to the center. They have a right to pre-school teaching and they are the only pre-school children in our country who have the legal right to such teaching from age two years up to 7 years of age. If the child can't come to the regular pre-school class and be integrated with normal children and handicapped children, the parents have the right to home teaching, wherein a teacher comes to the home and gives the child lessons about five hours a week.

Now, we have not found that this program gives such tremendous results that we can convince the politicians that this is so much cheaper to do, so we must support the programs we have of all different types. That is, we must not only think of institutions as politicians always want to do -- to see things built -- especially if they go up in the air! They always want to come and dedicate these houses and be proud of themselves with this small gesture! You in this country are fantastic in your small memorials, you know! We in Sweden are trying to rid ourselves of this attitude. We want to change the public attitude so that they will believe that the severe-profoundly retarded children and adults are able to live among us. For example, we have special books about handicapped children and their lives -- about all different types of handicapped children, even fat children and aggressive children since they are also a type of handicapped child. The books also discuss the immigrant children that we have from Korea and Yugoslavia, and thus the books look at different forms of prejudice. Then there is a book for the next stage in these normal children's reading ability. These are new and it is hoped that every child in our forthcoming generations will come up with attitudes different from what you and I and the children of today have, that is: attitudes other than prejudice about the handicapped.

In addition, we stress integrated classes for the trainable,

severe, and profoundly retarded children with normal children.
All children who are able to live with their parents have the right
to come to the class for trainables, and no one can be excluded
from that class. One third of these classes are integrated during
the day into schools for normal children. This is a tremendous
program for the other children -- for them to see the very handicapped children playing at the same playground and being together
with them. They are all going to the same schools, in the same
buses and playing on the same playgrounds. There were naturally
many doubts about this integration at the start of the program from
the parents' associations, from the headmasters of the schools,
and from others -- but it has been a success! We have found that
the fear that these children might be teased and tormented by the
others has turned into just the reverse. They were all overpro-
tected and helped too much by the other children. Headmasters
tell us that their teachers find that after one year of this type of
integration, the normal children have changed their attitude towards the handicapped children and they are more calm and less
restless. They are more sincere. The whole atmosphere in the
school has settled down as a result of what they have seen. Now
there are other children who are really helpless and still, they

278

can function. It is as if our normal children, for the first time

in their lives, had realized another dimension of living. There

are other things besides being the best in the class. They have

seen children who cannot speak or walk -- another tremendous

experience which we wanted all of our children to be a part of.

Mrs. Una Haynes

I would like to talk a little about mini-teams. If you are in-

terested, I am obtaining a grant to publish the revised curriculum

and that should be done this year. The curriculum will be backed

up by slides and films of improvised equipment and other kinds of

media whereby we hope to interest some of our University-Affili-

ated Facilities who have a good bio-clinical approach, since we

would like to train more personnel for these teams and thus make

them more available on a national scale. The "baby" programs

are working again on the cross-disciplinary model and now we are

in our first real operational year -- last year was a planning year.

We have had some input from people who have lived and worked in

the Scandanavian countries and I hope this has been helpful. We

have been trying to give a tremendous amount of support to the

Scandanavian ideas but we haven't had the discipline in the homes

as yet and maybe we need to learn more there. In the early days, the parents seemed to vocalize the problem of feeding the child during the first months the most. It is the daily kind of thing. For example, when he cries a good deal -- the comfort measures. This business of tube feeding has certainly turned off parents -- they can't get the girls over for tea when they have to haul out the hose! The nurses would end up in the bathroom because the kids were either constipated or had diarrhea or something like that -- these were the kinds of things that they seemed to have earlier in the program, and needed help with these daily sort of tasks. I do not know whether you are finding the same kind of challenges in your programs. We have to make available the programs and equipment for each of these curricula at a training center for others who would be interested.

Several times I have had the great pleasure of visiting some of your models downstate in Lincoln and Hastings, and some of the parallels to the ENCOR models. I found that a couple of things reinforced what Dr. Grunewald discussed earlier. There was one little girl there who was not yet 14 months old. Her family was told to place her in Beatrice when she was a year old. It really was wonderful to see what your colleagues were doing with her. The kid was really turned on, you know, but they cannot get this family to do anything because they had accepted this initial "hopeless"

280

prognosis, and they turned her off and they can't get them turned back on. So, the next thing that usually is suggested is a foster home. Yet, the family has great guilt in having this child in a foster family unless we put her in Timbuktu or some place like that. I was only on the periphery of the discussions on this child, but I was touched by it even this year. You know, this kind of thing can and still does happen!

Another thing I have been wondering about is whether we had teams available, mobile ones, for the beginning of the integration of the cerebral palsied... if it would be helpful to go out and work with the teacher or group who has just now begun to take on young-sters who have significant neuro-motor or other kinds of related handicaps. Would this be helpful -- to have them available on a community level? I think that we are beginning to do this with the babies. However, we develop a primary approach out of the mini-teams; not all five descend on the family at once. But I believe that they would be useful to direct-care people out in the field.

I suppose that this is a characteristic of human beings, but I soon discovered that when you go in as a mini-team member, that you had better go in and not just talk to people, but roll up your sleeves and put your actions where your mouth is! If you

can't feed them, don't expect anybody else to. At least, that is
the way that we are oriented and we have teams that operate
that way. I am happy, frankly, because I have heard that we
have been getting a great deal of feedback from the AAMD Pre-
Conference Course on the multiple-modality approach, and we
have rejoiced in our troika approach. If this is true, and if
some of our new found colleagues are in the University Affiliated
Facilities next year, we will insist that there be a heavy clinical
approach right there to do this kind of training. Maybe the first
thing we can do is to prepare such Facilities to teach other teams
this way.

There are emotional complaints that go along with this sort
of thing so that you can't just preach to parents how to better
things, you have got to recognize that there will be emotions
there. In our experience, the parents got talked to an awful lot
and we thought that maybe we could come in and listen carefully
to what they had to say and then help them with "hand-help". I
have often gotten closer to a patient by bathing his feet than by
any directive communication skills. Maybe I am old-fashioned.
I am very grateful to Dr. Pearson and his colleagues for accepting a small grant from the United Cerebral Palsy because it is

important that we find these babies earlier -- and let the family vocalize what they see when they feel something is wrong -- this provides for excellent early identification and early intervention approaches.

We are putting together a series of slide films to go with this new curriculum, and we will have a total package. Meanwhile, the techniques and approaches can be picked up in bits and pieces. For example, there's a publication called, "Teaching the Mentally Retarded Child", published by the Southern Education Board in which we have a couple of chapters. The Finny book has a practicum that describes techniques for the handicapped child at home. A new equipment manual is coming out soon, since there is a pressing need for same.

Dr. Grunewald

I find that we talk a good deal about children and although that is nice, we have so many adults who are also severe-profoundly retarded. I want this to be mentioned. This is such a bad situation and it can't be neglected. We naturally can't introduce the intensive type of stimulation and care for these adults that we have shown for the children, but we must use those methods which are available for this age group. I am thinking of those individuals who are 25 to 30 years of age. First, we can normalize their environment. Second, provide an environment which is close to the community so that at least, they are able to sit in the window and look out to see things happening. There is a lot of stimulation to be gained from such a set of experiences.

Also, living in a small group gives them the opportunity to express themselves. For example, we have found that aggressive behavior, which many of these severe-profoundly retarded individuals have (even those with physical handicaps), is very often a sickness which they can't explain. They can't seem to react in a natural way, but when they are placed into the environment of a small group, it has a large positive effect on their behavior.

I also think that we have to be very careful when choosing the personnel who will work with our adults. I speak more than anyone else in my country about demolishing institutions, but at the same time I feel we should save the personnel. Try to re-educate them and give them new hope. Try to put them on a new track. I know it isn't easy, but there is so much to save in them.

Speaking of institutions, I think we should be careful from a semantic point of view in stating what is an institution. You can have what you call a "Center" here... and it is an institution and nothing else; and what you can call "the hospital", is also an institution of sorts. We should have a more precise definition of of the concept, "Institution". For me personally, the word institution symbolized the meaning of isolation, including isolation from the community, and isolation from others. It is a type of colony where they have just their own lives and passive care, etc. I am not sure that what we call residential homes are not institutions. I would like our psychologists to help give us a better definition and tell us what it's like in the closed environment for the child or adult.

We haven't built any homes for the handicapped children in Sweden for the past 12 years which are more than one story in height. We, in Sweden, have this "primitive" belief that the human should be in contact with that which is green and with that which is happening on the ground. We aren't very interested in going up into the air, as you are here in America.

I would like to comment on the FOKUS approach to apartments. It is a program in Sweden through which we build special purpose houses, in the design of a small villa on the ground floor, as living quarters for physically handicapped adults who are not especially mentally retarded or at least they are trained enough so that they are as independent as possible. They have their own big apartments or rooms in the villa and they live 4 or 5 together in one villa. They rent the rooms. Many of them are very physically handicapped and are on the society programs with full wages and this is really their home. They are supported by personnel who do not live in the house but who give them all the help that they need. The villa is, of course, built with all the technical aids that these very physically handicapped people need. This is like a normal apartment house. I must add that when you have a program like this, you must be very certain that the handicapped individuals who will live there are adjusted so that they can be really independent. Otherwise we are normalizing them to a thing which is, perhaps, worse than they came from.

As to training personnel to help the retarded, last year we started an educational program for all of our youngsters who are 16 to 19 years of age, that is a total program for all and about 80% of our youngsters go to one of these branches of the schools. One of these 21 branches is a branch which trains you to be an aid or nurse in any type of child care. It starts with a very broad and generalized half year. After the half year, they select if they want to work with healthy or sick children. In another six months, they change work again and decide if they want to work with handicapped, blind or mentally retarded children. We call this a form of pyramid education. The pyramid is that you specialize more and more. However, it is a legal right in Sweden that no youngster should be stopped in his education, so if they want to they can always apply for further education. Our physicians, for example, will be selected from those who do their career from this pyramid education.

I could add to this that the 21 branches extend from the most theoretical ones to the most practical. We counsel our youth as to which area(s) they will choose for a future career. We, in mental retardation, were afraid that we would not have enough personnel in the hospitals, that the youngsters would choose academic training. But we found that they wanted to come over to this training where they could do something for humans. So we have relatively more than we thought we would get, since so many choose this line.

Let me give you an idea of a modern trend that we have started for severe and profoundly retarded children. It's a free-of-cost course provided for the parents of these children which enables them to live together at a summer residence for two weeks and obtain instruction and training to prepare them to keep their children at home. It is most often 8 to 10 parents together and they are given the same training as our personnel in the institutions.

We feel that they must know exactly as much as the personnel.
After all, who should know more than the children's parents! We
have this now as a program and I hope that it will work out well.
I present it to you as an idea if you are interested.

We have two basic types of developmental education programs
for the severe and profoundly retarded, and we must decide where
the child fits in. We must always cooperate with the parents; we
can't do anything against the parents' wishes, they have the last
word. If the parents wish, we will go into the class which has the
more academic programming. They have the right to request this
type of approach -- up to the point when they are convinced that
this is not good for the child and then he is transferred to another
group. This is in cooperation with the parents and the teachers
and the physician. Accordingly, there are always three persons
who decide these matters -- thus reflecting the true partnerships
that are directly needed for maximizing human development. The
professionals and the advocates of the retarded must work together
to provide new vistas of hope in the enlarging horizons of help for
severe-profoundly retarded citizens.

69329